The Vertical Hour

David Hare is one of Britain's most internationally performed playwrights. He was born in Sussex in 1947. Thirteen of his plays have been presented at the National Theatre, including a trilogy about the Church, the Law and the Labour Party – *Racing Demon, Murmuring Judges* and *The Absence of War* – which was presented in repertory in the Olivier Theatre in 1993. Ten of his best-known plays, including *Plenty, The Secret Rapture, Skylight, The Blue Room, Amy's View, The Judas Kiss, Via Dolorosa* – in which he performed – and *The Vertical Hour* have also been presented on Broadway.

DAVID HARE

The Vertical Hour

faber and faber

First published Great Britain in 2008
by Faber and Faber Limited
3 Queen Square, London WC1N 3AU

Typeset by Country Setting, Kingsdown, Kent CT14 8ES
Printed in the UK by CPI Bookmarque, Croydon, CR0 4TD

A CIP record for this book
is available from the British Library

ISBN 978-0-571-23352-6

2 4 6 8 10 9 7 5 3 1

For Nicole, always

The Vertical Hour received its first British production at the Royal Court Theatre, London, on 17 January 2008. The cast was as follows:

Oliver Lucas Anton Lesser
Nadia Blye Indira Varma
Dennis Dutton Joseph Kloska
Philip Lucas Tom Riley
Terri Scholes Wunmi Mosaku

Director Jeremy Herrin
Designer Mike Britton
Lighting Howard Harrison
Sound Nick Powell

The Vertical Hour had its world premiere on 30 November 2006 at the Music Box Theater, New York City. The cast was as follows:

Oliver Lucas Bill Nighy
Nadia Blye Julianne Moore
Dennis Dutton Dan Bittner
Philip Lucas Andrew Scott
Terri Scholes Rutina Wesley

Director Sam Mendes
Set Designer Scott Pask
Costume Designer Ann Roth
Lighting Designer Brian MacDevitt

Characters

Oliver Lucas
Nadia Blye
Dennis Dutton
Philip Lucas
Terri Scholes

THE VERTICAL HOUR

We need, in love, to practise
only this: letting each other go.
For holding on comes easily;
we do not need to learn it.

Rainer Maria Rilke

Act One

ONE

Oliver Lucas, alone. He is English, undemonstrative, casually dressed, in his late fifties.

Oliver I'd known for a long time I was going to have an accident. That's how it felt. The effort of concentration becomes impossible. For so many years you haven't made a mistake. Then you make one. It feels inevitable. You signal right, intending to go left. And you pay the price.

TWO

Nadia Blye is sitting at the desk in her office. She is American, pale, poised, in her mid-thirties, her style casual. Opposite her is Dennis Dutton, in his early twenties, also American. He is unusually dressed for someone of his age, in suit and tie, with floppy hair and trainers.

Nadia This is not a bad essay.

Dutton Thank you.

Nadia It's not bad.

Dutton waits.

This is our last class together. Clearly, I haven't persuaded you to my view of politics.

Dutton I know your view.

Nadia It's competing claims, isn't it? If I had to sum it up.

Dutton That's your view.

Nadia That's right. People want different things. The things they want can't be reconciled. Not everyone can *have* what they want. So the mediation between the groups, between the interest groups, the groups who want different things, to that process we give the name 'politics'.

Nadia waits, but there's no reply.

Ultimately, you could say, politics is about the reconciliation of the irreconcilable.

Dutton I don't see it that way.

Nadia No.

Dutton For me, politics is about the protection of property and of liberty.

Nadia Yes, that's what you seem to be saying in this essay.

Dutton It *is* what I'm saying. It's about peoples' rights to live their own lives. It's about absolutes.

Nadia thinks, considering how to go about this.

Nadia Yes. Yes, but there's a problem, isn't there?

Dutton Is there?

Nadia We know for a fact that human life by its nature tends towards unfairness.

Dutton Do we know that?

Nadia So: checks and balances have to be introduced. By human agency. The state, in any system yet proposed by man – be it communism, be it capitalism – has to intervene to balance things out.

Dutton I don't accept the term.

Nadia What term?

Dutton 'Capitalism'.

Nadia frowns.

Nadia You don't accept the term?

Dutton No.

Nadia You don't accept it?

Dutton No.

Nadia Meaning? Meaning what?

Dutton I don't think there's any such thing.

Nadia No such thing as capitalism?

Dutton Correct.

Nadia So what name do you give it then? The system
we live under today? The system we call 'consumer
capitalism', 'liberal democracy', characterised by political
parties and – I don't know – huge corporations, massively
powerful industrial and military interests? The system as
evolved by the West, by Western democracies? What do
you call it?

Dutton Life. I call it 'life'.

Nadia nods slightly.

Nadia No offence, but do you think Political Studies was
a good choice of subject for you?

Dutton My father wanted me to do it.

Nadia He's important to you?

Dutton Very much so. I admire him more than anyone in
the world.

Nadia looks a moment, thoughtful.

Nadia It's just . . . how do I put this? Basic to Political Studies is the notion of comparison.

Dutton Sure.

Nadia We compare.

Dutton Sure.

Nadia That's what we do. We say, 'Here's one way at looking at things, now here's another.'

Dutton So?

Nadia Well, such comparison becomes difficult if we start out with the idea that there's only one system – there's only one way.

Dutton But there is.

Nadia Is there?

Dutton I know it's inconvenient to ask, but why do you think America has triumphed?

Nadia is slightly thrown.

Nadia Inconvenient? Is 'inconvenient' the word for America's triumph? And I'm not sure I'm going to go with 'triumph' either.

Dutton Why not? Why not 'triumph'?

Nadia Listen. Listen. This is a school. It's not a madrasa. We're not teaching one path. We're teaching many paths. You say you admire liberal democracy. Well, basic to liberal democracy is the idea of free discussion. The free exchange of ideas. *Comparison.*

Dutton You telling me I'm wrong to love America?

Nadia I'm not.

Dutton I'm wrong to love my country?

6

Nadia No. I'm not telling you any such thing. I'm telling you not to be blinded by love, that's all. Not to be made stupid by love.

Dutton Stupid?

Nadia, embarrassed, picks up his essay and walks to the other side of the room. Dutton is seen to pluck up courage.

The fact is – I haven't wanted to say – I've come here to say this today: it's you I'm in love with.

Nadia It's me?

Dutton I don't eat. I don't sleep. Ever since we met. Ever since – you must have noticed.

Nadia What, that –

Dutton I've lost weight alarmingly. Have you noticed?

Nadia I haven't.

Dutton I'm sick. I went to a barbecue on the weekend. The smell repelled me.

Nadia is lost for a response.

I think of you all the time. I find the idea of you incredibly exciting. Of who you are.

Nadia Who I am? Say. If you imagine . . . For goodness' sake. Let's be serious! Tell me. Who am I?

Dutton This woman out there in the world.

Nadia What woman?

Dutton On television.

Dutton immediately holds up a hand.

All right, that was a foolish thing to say.

Nadia A tad.

Dutton It's not what I meant . . .

Nadia You have feelings for me because I've been on television?

Dutton A woman in the world. That's what I mean. A woman in the world.

After the shock, Nadia is now angry.

Nadia Dennis, Dennis, I have to tell you there are now quite a lot of women in the world. As you put it. Quite a lot. In fact, the whole assumption dismays me. How old are you?

Dutton Twenty-two.

Nadia I'm a feminist and what you're saying dismays me.

Dutton Why?

Nadia Because the purpose of women taking part, the purpose of women being intelligent or public or in any way *represented* even, the purpose of women talking on television about international politics is not to turn men on!

There is a silence. Dutton is very quiet.

Dutton You didn't know? You had no idea?

Nadia I'm going to ignore what you said. I'm going to forget it.

There is a brief silence.

Dutton Can I say something?

Nadia If it's about politics, yes.

Dutton It's all nonsense, isn't it?

Nadia I don't know what's nonsense. You tell me.

Dutton The study of international relations.

Nadia In what way is it nonsense, Dennis?

Dutton I took this course – as you know, I'm a business major, my interest is start-up – but my father wanted me to broaden my mind. I don't know why. Dad's own mind is about as narrow as it's possible to be.

Nadia Narrow, how?

Dutton He wants money. That's the only thing he wants.

Nadia Well?

Dutton sits forward.

Dutton This is my point: America wins. It always wins. You can do all that historical perspective stuff, you can say it's an empire and like any empire it's going to fall. But not yet it isn't. Not in my lifetime. So. Say there's a runner – the runner wins the race – then the other runners, if they're at all intelligent, they ask, 'How did he do that?' They look at the winner, they look at his methods, they analyse, they say 'OK'. And that's the way other countries are going to prosper. They'll prosper by imitating America. And to me that's Political Studies. 'What does America do? And how can anyone else get close?'

Nadia Well, I'm glad my year of teaching hasn't been entirely wasted.

Dutton It hasn't been wasted.

Nadia Good.

Dutton In fact . . .

Nadia Dennis . . .

Dutton That's what I wanted to say. I didn't want you to think I took this course – well, for any other reason but in order to learn. The last thing I want is to upset you.

Nadia Thank you.

Dutton You're a brilliant teacher.

Nadia looks wary, fearing what comes next.

However, we can't . . . Face it – the other thing happened to me.

Nadia Dennis . . .

Dutton It happened. I can't pretend it didn't. I fell in love. In fact, the other day, I might as well tell you, I was talking things over with my fiancée . . .

Nadia I'm sorry? Your fiancée? *I'm sorry?*

Nadia throws up her hands, exasperated.

Dutton Look, just so you understand . . .

Nadia I don't. In fact, I don't want to understand.

Now it is Dutton's turn to get up, agitated.

Dutton It's not – it's hard – listen! *Listen!* I don't know if you don't – if you know Maine – anyway, two big families. In our part of the state. Big families. Both – whatever. And for many years, it's been assumed, if you like. Everyone takes it for granted. I will end up with Val. Understand.

Nadia I just said: I don't want to understand.

Dutton But just so you know. So you know the context. Let me say: Val is not just my fiancée, she's also a friend. Val is my best friend.

Nadia And Val has no problem juggling these two roles?

Dutton Val – talking to Val is like talking to someone – someone objective. And it was Val who said, she said, 'Look, Dennis, you're suffering. You have been suffering.

For a long time. For your own sake, you must speak to her.' It was she who suggested it. Not me.

Nadia looks at Dutton, trying to work him out. Then she goes and sits on the far side of the room, as if defeated.

I wouldn't be saying this. I wouldn't be saying it if it were up to me.

There is a silence. When Nadia answers she is hesitant.

What are you thinking?

Nadia I suppose one imagines – I imagine – the world moves forward. Slowly, the world moves forward. My assumption has always been that society would progress. I work on that assumption. Old attitudes die out. But what can you say? They don't. They don't.

Dutton I'm not sure I understand you.

Nadia As you know, I spend a lot of time in war zones – in Bosnia, in Serbia. In many ways I can only say I prefer it there. I prefer being there because here people –

Nadia changes tack, not finishing her thought.

Put it another way: I am so far from regarding myself as somebody available to a twenty-two-year-old as not to recognise myself in the description.

Dutton But that's good, isn't it? Isn't that a good thing?

There is a silence.

Nadia This has been a profoundly depressing few minutes.

Dutton looks at her a moment.

Dutton I hear you.

Nadia Good.

Dutton But nothing you say convinces me. As it happens, before I took politics, I took psychology . . .

Nadia Oh Christ!

Dutton Briefly. Freud.

Nadia How many weeks? How many weeks did you study Freud?

Dutton Three. Intensely.

Nadia Sure.

Dutton Actually you can understand quite a lot in three weeks.

Nadia You can also misunderstand quite a lot in three weeks.

Dutton Do you know this?

Nadia Try me.

Dutton Freud has a theory that we aren't who we claim to be.

Nadia Really?

Dutton Freud says we're all somebody else. Underneath. Underneath.

Nadia I would have thought that was self-evident. I would have thought that was obvious.

Dutton Maybe it is obvious, but have you considered what it means?

Nadia Clearly, you're going to tell me I haven't.

Dutton leans forward, intent.

Dutton Think: the real person – the person concealed – is quite different, has quite different feelings from the person on the surface.

Nadia Well, it's a highly convenient theory. But that's all it is. A theory.

Dutton So what I'm getting at is this: you don't convince me. And something tells me – my own instincts tell me – that underneath you don't even convince yourself.

Nadia tries not to be angry.

I think this has happened before. I'm not the first student, am I? I know. I know you won't tell me. But I'm guessing it happens all the time. I don't see how it can't. It must. And yet for some reason you pretend it doesn't.

Nadia just looks at him.

I've got a feeling that's part of your attraction.

This is the last straw for Nadia. She goes to open the door for him to leave.

Nadia That's it. That's the end of the course. Here is your essay.

Dutton Is that it? Are we finished?

Nadia We're finished.

Dutton Thank you very much.

Nadia No. Thank *you*.

Nadia has given him the essay at the door, and now they have shaken hands.

I believe I began by saying politics is about irreconcilable differences. So, by that standard, we've just had a terrific political discussion.

Dutton Yes.

Dutton waits a moment.

What are my chances of seeing you again?

Nadia They're zero.

Dutton nods, accepting.

Up until now I would have dismissed you as a sort of throwback, Dennis.

Dutton Would you?

Nadia In all sorts of ways.

Dutton I don't see why.

Nadia You're going into the world of money, is that right? The world of finance.

Dutton I'm going into my father's business.

Nadia Maybe it's my ignorance, but I don't believe that world will be different from any other. The most important thing you can take into it is an open mind.

Dutton looks at her a moment.

Dutton Why? Why would I want an open mind?

Nadia Why would you not?

Dutton Our enemies don't have open minds.

THREE

Nadia, alone.

Nadia It's a choice, isn't it? How you live. How you behave. You make a choice. At some point in your life you think: there must be an intelligent way to live. And you make your choice. Maybe you don't even remember. Everything conspires to make you forget. But the choice is there. You made it.

FOUR

A lawn looking over the Welsh and English countryside.
A tree. A blissful, sunny day. There are canvas chairs.
The remains of breakfast. Both Oliver and Philip are in
shirtsleeves. Philip Lucas is English, in his early thirties,
notably handsome.

Oliver So tell me, tell me a little, so I know something
about her before we meet.

Philip Aside from beautiful and brilliant?

Oliver Aside from that, yes.

Philip smiles, thinking of her.

Philip Formidable, certainly. Committed. Articulate.
Passionate. Full of strong feeling.

Oliver OK. Enough of her faults, now tell me her virtues.

Philip Well, the first time I met her she was carrying a
book. *Pas de psychologie, pas de psychose.*

Oliver What did that mean?

Philip 'No psychology, no psychosis.'

Oliver No, I know what it means. I know what it means.
I'm not an idiot. Choosing that book.

Philip All right, Dad.

Oliver That's what I'm asking. What did that mean?

Philip thinks a moment.

Philip Well. As you know, Nadia teaches at Yale . . .

Oliver I know that . . .

Philip Obviously what she was trying to say is that she
isn't keen on the psychological.

Oliver I see.

Philip She has a horror of it. I thought: that's refreshing. That's such a refreshing approach.

Oliver Why? Why did you think that?

Philip Oh. Because the first thing you notice, it becomes a way of life. People are taught to say 'I think, I feel.' They talk all the time as if there were no such thing as reality.

Oliver Really?

Philip Or rather: they know reality exists, they know it's there, but they can't help believing that what they feel about it is somehow more important than reality itself.

Oliver You're talking about Americans?

Philip Not only. But obviously. Having spent time there.

Oliver It's something you've noticed?

Philip Say you have an experience. Any experience. You're walking along the street and a man drops dead in front of you. And people's first response is 'Really? A man dropped dead in the street? How did that make you feel?'

Oliver That's funny.

Philip Yeah, but it's decadent, isn't it? As if it's not the world, it's not the world you're interested in, it's just your own reaction to it.

Oliver looks at him.

Oliver Huh.

Philip I'll give you another example. This is an interesting example. Take the former Yugoslavia. If you remember just a few years ago . . .

Oliver I do remember . . .

Philip Yugoslavia falling apart, on the verge of collapse. But Nadia told me that before she first went out there, she mentioned to someone, 'You know, I think this is really important.' Whereupon the person looked at her and said, 'Have you noticed, you seem quite emotional, Nadia? Have you ever stopped and asked yourself *why*? Why you're so worked up? All this fascination with foreign trouble spots, have you ever considered there might be a reason? Has it occurred to you, you may just be running away from problems in your own life?'

Philip smiles at the absurdity of the question.

Oliver Well?

Philip Well, what?

Oliver How did Nadia reply? *Did* Nadia have problems?

Philip No, I don't think so. Not that she's told me about.

They both smile.

No, on the contrary. Nadia replied, 'I'm not going to Yugoslavia because there's anything wrong with me. I'm going because there's something wrong in Yugoslavia. It's called ethnic cleansing. And it exists.'

Philip laughs.

It's crazy. It's ridiculous, isn't it?

Oliver To be honest, I can't imagine.

Philip Why not?

Oliver Because the people who need me so obviously need me.

Nadia comes out onto the lawn.

Philip Ah, there you are.

Oliver Good morning.

Nadia reaches out a hand.

Nadia Hello.

Oliver Oliver.

Nadia I'm sorry, Philip. I overslept. I didn't realise you'd got up.

Philip I got up.

Oliver Good. Well this is charming, charming.

Nadia Good morning.

Nadia kisses Philip. They all stand a moment, embarrassed.

Oliver So. Let me – right – to give you the idea, has anyone explained?

Nadia No.

Oliver This is border country. That way, the sea. That way, the south.

Nadia Toward the sun.

Oliver Precisely.

Nadia Goodness, I really did oversleep.

Philip It's not like you.

Nadia It isn't.

Philip You always wake so early.

Oliver You drove through the night, so I don't know how much you saw. Philip said you'd only been to England once before.

Philip For a conference.

Nadia At Chatham House. International relations. It was brief.

Oliver smiles formally.

Oliver It's rare as you know for Philip to visit me at all, let alone in company.

Nadia Actually it was an impulse. It was an impulsive thing.

Oliver Whose impulse?

Philip Both of us.

Oliver Hence the short notice.

Philip We got cheap tickets.

Nadia Some of the happiest times we've had together, doing things on the spur of the moment.

Philip Very much so.

They both smile.

Nadia We simply got up one morning and decided we needed a vacation. Please don't read anything into it.

Oliver I haven't.

Philip God forbid.

Nadia Philip and I had both been working very hard.

Philip It's something that happens over there. It's in the culture. You find yourself working every day of the year.

Oliver Really?

Nadia And Philip said it was silly that I'd barely visited the country where he was born.

Oliver Or the people he was born to?

Nadia Those too.

Oliver You're meeting both of us?

Philip Yes.

Oliver Better and better. The grand tour.

Again, Oliver smiles icily.

I'm being very rude. Let me get you some breakfast.

Nadia In a moment. Yes. Thank you.

Philip Or shall I do it?

Oliver Philip has actually tried to tell me what you do. I can't say I understand it entirely.

Philip Oh, Dad . . .

Oliver What?

Philip For God's sake!

Nadia I'm not sure I do either.

Philip Putting Nadia on the spot.

Oliver I'm not putting her on the spot. I'm making conversation.

Philip That's even worse!

Oliver Even: I'm *interested.*

Philip She's only just got up.

Nadia I can't believe you want a lecture from me.

Oliver I'm not asking for a lecture. I'm asking for enlightenment.

Nadia OK.

Oliver Thank you.

They all smile. It's easier.

Nadia I teach politics. That's what I do. It's what I always wanted to do.

Oliver From when you were young?

Nadia Exactly. In fact, I remember –

Oliver Yes?

Nadia Even at school, I remember being bewildered. So much time spent reading – I don't know – medieval literature, doing trigonometry, when meanwhile all the important things were being ignored.

Oliver What were they?

Nadia All right: why so many people live in such poverty. And so few live well. And what can we do about it? These huge facts, these enormous facts not up for study. Ignored. You'd think that to be alive would mean to want to find out.

Oliver looks at her a moment.

Oliver But specifically . . .

Nadia Yes?

Oliver Philip had suggested . . .

Nadia Yes?

Oliver Your area is now international relations?

Nadia That's right.

Oliver Your specific concern.

Nadia My field.

Oliver With a particular interest in terror.

Nadia Oh, no, not 'particular'.

Oliver I read on the internet: you're known as the professor of terror.

Philip That's what she has to put up with.

Nadia Only in the media. And among a few of my students. The dumber ones.

Oliver Do you have stupid students?

Nadia I'm afraid I do. Or at least I was thinking before I left.

Oliver Why? Why before you left?

Nadia Oh. Something that happened. A student. My God. Made me think.

Nadia smiles.

Philip Excuse me. I'm going to get coffee.

Philip goes out.

Oliver But you have written about terror?

Nadia Of course. Everyone does. You can't do what I do and not be fascinated by it.

Oliver waits for her to go on.

All right, crudely, if you're asking, you can say, if you want to put it this way, that terrorism may be the wrong answer to the right question.

Oliver What question is that?

Nadia Well, I'd have thought terror's an attack on modernity, isn't it?

Oliver I'm never sure. Tell me what 'modernity' means.

Nadia Usually it means that human beings feel themselves discontented, they feel lost in the world – if there's nothing *but* the world – and they imagine that materialism must therefore be at fault.

Nadia shifts.

Of course – look, not to insult you – it's much more complicated than that . . .

Oliver Of course . . .

Nadia And the actual *motivation* –

Oliver Yes . . .

Nadia – the moment at which an individual picks up a gun, or straps on explosives – that moment is still deeply obscure. People claim to understand it, but do they? I certainly don't. But underlying that desire you'll often find the same discontent: namely, the conviction that materialism isn't enough.

Oliver And is that what you think?

Nadia People blame materialism because they feel it doesn't nourish them. And you could say, it's true: materialism, by definition, isn't heroic. In the West, you no longer become famous for what you do, simply for what happens to you. We celebrate victims, not heroes. We're infantilised by fear to a point where all we want is to live as long and comfortably as possible. And so this Western ethic of survival, merely surviving as a human being – as though the world were everything, and the manner in which you live in it unimportant – seems to other people, other cultures, well . . . ignoble.

Oliver Do you agree?

Nadia Me?

Oliver Is that your own view? Do you feel that?

Nadia looks at him a moment.

Nadia I don't know. But, whether it is or not, the answer isn't violence.

Philip appears on the lawn.

Philip I'm assuming you want toast.

Nadia Yes, please.

Philip Honey or jam?

Nadia Honey. No, jam. Honey.

Philip I'll bring both.

Philip goes. Nadia remembers after he's gone.

Nadia Thanks, babe!

Oliver In fact, I must admit when I went to your website –

Nadia Oh, that . . .

Oliver It lists subjects about which you're available to speak.

Nadia It's a fancy piece of publicity. Shaming, but you have to do it.

Oliver Do you?

Nadia Sure.

Oliver Why's that?

Nadia Being an academic isn't quite what it was. We find ourselves doing all sorts of things.

Oliver I see.

Nadia Inevitably, yes, I talk to the media.

Oliver You make a point of it?

Nadia looks a moment, detecting criticism.

Nadia My special privilege has been to define my job as I go along. The university's been very generous.

Oliver You're free?

Nadia That's it.

Oliver Free to do what you choose?

Nadia More or less.

Oliver Because of your status?

Nadia If you choose to put it like that. I barely teach. Mostly, I write.

Oliver Philip said there was a book.

Nadia There is. And I'm writing another. This is a relatively new study. Or rather it's an old study which has been transformed. Am I boring you?

Oliver No.

Nadia You'll let me know if I'm boring you?

Oliver You're not.

Nadia As long as we had two great powers, two superpowers in some sort of balance, then there seemed to be a procedure for determining the world's affairs.

Oliver Now there's only one.

Nadia Exactly. So my area of study becomes more vital.

Oliver Especially after Iraq.

Nadia As you say. Yes. Especially after Iraq.

Nadia looks again, trying to gauge his agenda. Then she gets up and moves to look out over the hills.

I didn't get much of a look last night, but this wasn't what I was expecting.

Oliver This spot?

Nadia Yes.

Oliver In what way?

Nadia I knew you were alone. But still.

Oliver I am alone.

Nadia Is that a choice?

Oliver Well, this place would hardly be chance, would it?

Nadia How do you pronounce it?

Oliver Shrewsbury.

They smile together.

I came here over ten years ago.

Nadia As long as that? And you don't mind? You don't mind the isolation?

Oliver Philip was already practising. He'd gone, he'd left home.

Nadia His mother brought him up?

Oliver Officially, yes. But I did my share. You haven't met her yet?

Oliver gestures round.

There aren't many spots left where you can turn three hundred and sixty degrees and see barely a single building.

Nadia You went out of your way?

Oliver In France they have this expression. '*France profonde*'.

Nadia I'm embarrassed. I don't speak French.

Oliver No? I'm surprised.

Nadia Why? Why does that surprise you?

Oliver Oh. Something Philip said.

Nadia What was that?

Oliver is reluctant.

No, say.

Oliver *Pas de psychologie, pas de psychose.*

There is a moment. Nadia seems displeased.

Nadia He told you that? Why did he tell you that?

Oliver I'm sorry, have I crossed some sort of line?

Nadia No, no, no.

Oliver Please, I didn't mean to upset you.

Nadia You haven't upset me.

Oliver I happened to ask him how you met, that's all.

Nadia turns away.

Nadia It's silly. Why do I want private things to be private?

Philip returns with coffee and toast for Nadia.

Philip You two all right?

Nadia We are. Thank you.

Oliver Fine.

Nadia takes her breakfast from him.

Nadia Obviously you and your dad were talking while I was asleep.

Philip Oh, not much.

Oliver No, no, no.

Philip Very little, in fact.

Oliver Philip's one of those people who's always been at peace with silence.

Philip Silence never bothered me.

Oliver If the world can be divided into those who need to speak and those who don't –

Philip People only talk because they're nervous.

Oliver It's funny. There's a doctor at the hospital who's notorious for his pauses. Ear, Nose and Throat. 'What are my chances, Doctor?' 'Well . . .'

Oliver pauses elaborately.

If the patient doesn't die of the disease, they die of suspense.

Nadia And you?

Oliver Me?

Nadia How's your manner?

Oliver Oh, reasonably sympathetic, I hope. Early on, they taught me something I try not to forget.

Nadia What's that?

Oliver The definition of a doctor.

Nadia I've never heard it. Tell me.

Oliver A doctor is someone who tells you the truth and stays with you to the end.

Nadia stops eating and looks directly at him.

Not bad, eh?

Nadia No. Not bad.

Oliver It's pretty good, isn't it?

Philip shifts, not sure what's going on.

Philip Are we going into town? I'd like to show Nadia the town.

Oliver takes no notice.

Oliver Nadia's been explaining how things have changed for the academic. The public role.

Nadia Your father sounds as if he disapproves.

Oliver Not at all.

Nadia As if it were vulgar.

Oliver Not vulgar, no. But I have my own idea of what it is to be a professional. The two requirements: to be objective and to be discreet.

Nadia I'd hope I was both of those.

Oliver looks at her a moment.

Oliver Philip mentioned . . . Philip did mention that the President asked for you.

Nadia He did. Believe it or not, he did.

Oliver You went to the White House?

Nadia I did.

Oliver Goodness.

Nadia I know.

Oliver What did he want?

Nadia Oh, you can imagine.

Oliver Actually, no. I have no idea.

Nadia He wanted briefing. He wanted advice.

Oliver Which you were able to give?

Nadia doesn't answer.

About Iraq?

Nadia Yes. He knew I'd written about Iraq.

Oliver Clearly you were in favour? You were in favour of the invasion?

Nadia The liberation, yes. Yes, I was in favour. I don't think the President would have asked me if I wasn't.

Oliver No.

They both smile.

Nadia Whatever you think, whatever your view, I'd have to say, it is undeniably something.

Oliver For you?

Nadia No, I'm not talking personally. I'm talking about entering. Walking in. It's impressive. You're picked up at your hotel in a black car, with blacked-out windows. Five minutes later you're standing on the carpet in the Oval Office.

Oliver It's theatre?

Nadia That's right. Theatre.

Nadia looks down, slightly embarrassed.

Also in our country, it isn't just the person, it's the office.

Oliver He's the President.

Nadia In America . . . in America that still means something.

Oliver Quite.

Nadia It really does. Do I sound naive?

Oliver I don't think so.

Nadia Because from what people tell me, it's not the same here.

Oliver Not in the smallest degree.

Nadia Why is that?

Oliver It's hard to explain. But I'm probably typical.

Philip Dad is absolutely typical.

Nadia How?

Philip smiles, dodging the question.

Philip I left this country, remember?

Oliver No doubt you feel that if your President calls, you have to answer that call. If my Prime Minister called, I'd let it ring. That's the difference.

Philip It's true.

Oliver And what's more, *what's more*, politics being what it is in this country – i.e., everything, *everything* – my Prime Minister wouldn't call me in the first place.

Philip That's definitely true.

Nadia Do you – I don't know how to ask this . . . Am I ridiculous for asking this?

Oliver Ask.

Nadia Does no one here have any concept of national loyalty? Of being part of a nation?

Oliver Oh.

Nadia Well?

Oliver I don't know how to answer. Like most people, I do have a button marked 'patriotism'. But – let's say –

I'm choosy about who I allow to press it. Certainly not politicians. And certainly not the Queen.

Nadia Who then?

Oliver Oh you know. Blake. Wilfred Owen.

Philip They're poets.

Nadia I know.

There's a silence. Nobody moves.

Oliver An appeal to patriotism is a contradiction in terms. Especially when made by politicians. You can no more appeal to patriotism than you can appeal to love. You may feel it, but you can't demand it. Wilfred Owen, yes. Fifty-seven thousand British casualties on the first morning on the Battle of the Somme, sent into a murderous war by the ruthless, out-of-touch political class of the day. People with no direct experience of war, and no knowledge of its reality, send ordinary working men to die on their behalf. They stay at home. The men die. Hello? Hard to explain, impossible to justify. And one man – one great man – adequate to describe the event.

Philip smiles to himself.

Philip Dad liked the Sex Pistols as well.

Oliver I admit it.

Philip Same reason.

Oliver Similar.

Philip All right . . .

Oliver Not the same.

Philip OK.

Oliver Don't make me sound stupid. But I did like the Sex Pistols.

Oliver sits back, expansive.

The only patriotic outfit still operating in this country is the awkward squad. In the United States, you're building an empire. Remember, we've dismantled one. When Philip was young I remember him saying he'd like to be gay or an immigrant because then he'd belong. He wanted a tribe.

Nadia Isn't medicine a tribe?

Oliver Used to be. Now it's freelance. We've been – what's the word? – outsourced. The politicians dismantle communities, then complain that community no longer exists. They incubate the disease, then profess to be shocked when people catch it. 'Oh, why can't people behave?' Well, why can't they? It's a good question. When the people who make the law become lawless themselves, what can you do? How can politicians lead except by example?

Nadia smiles, giving up.

Nadia You have a high standard.

Oliver Not that high.

Nadia If you're talking about what I think you're talking about.

Philip I don't think there's much doubt, is there?

Oliver I don't think there is.

Philip It's a fair chance, one way or another, Dad's returned to the subject of Iraq.

Oliver Gosh. How did you know?

Philip He usually does.

Oliver 'Usually'?

Philip All right . . .

Oliver I don't think, Philip, you're in a position to say 'usually'.

Philip I agree. I'm not.

Oliver 'Usually', when you never see me?

Philip OK . . .

Oliver Not just don't see me, barely ever talk, don't even talk to me.

Philip Whose fault is that?

Oliver I know. I'm just saying. For all that.

An edgy silence. Nadia puts her plate aside.

Nadia Good, well, maybe this is the moment to set off for Shrewsbury.

Oliver Maybe it is.

They smile at one another.

Nadia Believe me, if it's what you want, I'm happy to have the Iraq discussion.

Oliver I'm not asking for it.

Nadia I'll have it tonight if you want.

Oliver I'm not insisting.

Nadia I've had it every day for the last three years. I never supposed a vacation in England would be a vacation from the argument.

Oliver Quite.

Nadia Why should today be different?

Nadia gets up and turns, formal.

No doubt you can imagine, I've taken a huge amount of flak.

Oliver I'm sure.

Nadia In liberal Connecticut defending the war has not been a popular position.

Oliver It's not been big in Shropshire either.

Nadia If you're interested: I was quite clear about why I supported it. I'm also clear about what's gone wrong. And I don't think the extraordinary incompetence of what's followed invalidates the original decision. I've always supported humane intervention in countries where terrible things are happening. I believe in it. With all my heart. If the choice is between stepping in or staying put and watching dictators let rip, then I'm for stepping in. I was a reporter before I was as an academic. I've been in these places. I've seen suffering – at ground level. And I've been present in situations in which the West did nothing. I've seen the results of our indifference. So. If you want me to pass my evening defending the right of Western countries to use their muscle to free Arabs from systematic murder, believe me, I'm up for it.

Oliver I'm sure you are.

Nadia I take it you were against?

Oliver Passionately.

Nadia From the beginning?

Oliver Let's just say, I knew who the surgeon was going to be, so I had fair idea what the operation would look like.

Oliver gets up.

Please. Don't take it amiss. I'm not being rude.

Nadia I know that.

Oliver Least of all to you, to you of all people, Nadia. I'm thrilled my son has brought somebody home. Even if it isn't home. In the proper sense.

There's a moment. Oliver speaks quietly.

All I want is Philip's happiness.

Nadia We want the same thing.

Oliver And if you can contribute to that happiness, then believe me nobody could be more welcome.

There's a brief silence.

Nadia However.

Oliver I'm sorry?

Nadia I sense a 'however'.

Oliver No. There is no 'however'.

They look at each other a moment.

Nadia Excuse me. I'll get my things.

She goes off into the house. Philip moves away, Oliver doesn't move. A few moments go by.

Philip Can I just say: this is an act of trust. I trusted you!

Oliver Well?

Philip Dad, I didn't have to do this. I did it because I wanted to.

Oliver So?

There is a silence. Oliver says nothing.

Philip It's my own fault. I have this ridiculous need for family.

Oliver Why ridiculous?

Philip Apart from anything, because I'm the only person in my family who has it.

Oliver Your mother has it.

Philip throws him a mistrustful look.

Philip Just look at Nadia. You see what she is! You can tell what she is! This is the best piece of luck in my life! Meeting her! What, I'm not to marry her because you don't approve of her position on Iraq?

Oliver Come on, nobody said that.

Philip Didn't they?

Oliver Nobody put it like that.

Philip They didn't need to, did they?

Oliver And maybe I wasn't listening but I didn't hear anyone say 'marriage' either.

Philip is silent. Oliver is amused.

What am I meant to say? What have I done wrong?

Philip You know full well.

Oliver Do I?

Philip You could be a little more welcoming.

Oliver Welcoming?

Philip Yes.

Oliver Come on, it's been a good old Welsh borders welcome. What was missing? Conjuring tricks?

But Philip has already moved away.

Philip She said, 'I'd be fascinated to see a little family background.' It's not very easy, is it, to explain, 'Oh you can meet my father, but bear in mind, this is a man who destroyed my mother's life.'

Oliver Did I?

Philip And now – for reasons I'm not going into – he lives alone on a hillside, repelling boarders. Or rather, repelling male boarders.

Oliver smiles, unperturbed, enjoying himself.

Oliver Philip, this is a tense and unnatural situation.

Philip You could say.

Oliver Of course it is. It will test both of our characters to the limit.

Philip Very funny.

Oliver Neither of us – all right? – has too much experience of conventional family life.

Philip To put it no higher.

Oliver But, in my opinion, I think you're letting it get to you.

Oliver sits back, content.

You say she's the greatest piece of luck in your life.

Philip She is.

Oliver In that case, you might ask, why risk your luck by bringing her here to meet me?

Philip I'm beginning to ask that myself.

Oliver Well then, why did you?

Philip just looks at him.

All right. In fact, take one step back and I think you'll find the whole thing is going remarkably well.

Philip You think so?

Oliver She's enjoying my company and relishing the chance to talk to someone who's almost as clever as she is.

Philip You mean as opposed to me?

Oliver looks at him reproachfully.

Oliver Look, Philip, if you'd like a piece of advice –

Philip Advice from you?

Oliver – then I'd say, just from my experience – I have some experience of this – strategically it wouldn't be very clever when in Nadia's company to show self-doubt. Trust me. It would not be advantageous. Because – I admit, you know her better than I do – but my guess is that Nadia Blye is not someone who easily tolerates weakness. She doesn't *like* it. Am I right?

Philip doesn't answer.

Anyone who announces that psychology's a load of rubbish – well, you choose to call that attitude 'refreshing'. I think a better word for it might be 'dangerous'. That's all I'm saying.

Philip You've said enough.

Oliver Take one look at her: she's someone who'd have very little trouble attracting any man on campus.

Philip So?

Oliver So my guess is, she's picked you out because you appear to be strong. Well then. Be strong. Why disappoint her? As our government instructs us, be alert but not alarmed. Face it: nothing serious is going to go wrong unless you let it go wrong.

There is a mistrustful silence.

Philip We're here till tomorrow. We're here till tomorrow night.

Oliver Good. Then we'll all take it step by step and see how it goes.

Oliver examines his nails, smiling. Philip is annoyed with himself.

Philip And I don't feel self-doubt when I'm in America.

Oliver Good.

Philip I like American life.

Oliver I'm sure you do.

Philip I like the feel of it. The look. It suits me. In America, I stand with a gin and tonic, I look out of the window, people are going out to the mall, and I feel hopeful. Explain that.

Oliver I can't.

Philip The landscape moves me. Crazy, isn't it? When there's a road across the desert and nothing in sight. When it snows in New England. Sobbing like a child about a place which isn't even home.

Oliver looks down, mischievous.

Oliver Well it's always nice, isn't it, to get away from one's parents.

Philip In my case very much so.

Oliver And what's more with an American girlfriend. Though from what I read in the magazines American women can be quite exacting.

Philip turns, half amused, half exasperated.

Philip Oh God, are you off again?

Oliver Am I?

Philip Why do you do this? My whole life, you did this stuff. Did nobody tell you? Kids aren't meant to be objects of satire, you know. That's not why most people opt for parenthood.

Oliver No, you're right.

Philip Most people don't use their children to refine their jokes on.

Oliver I know. Absolutely.

Philip Well?

Oliver You're right. Of course you're right.

Philip You're fifty-eight. It's unbecoming.

Oliver I'll stop.

Nadia returns.

Philip Good, you're ready. I'll get the car keys.

Nadia I've got them here.

Nadia holds them out.

Are you coming with us?

Oliver I'm not. You enjoy yourselves.

Nadia hesitates, about to go.

Nadia I was thinking, something about this situation reminds me of J. Paul Getty. Do you know who I mean?

Oliver Of course.

Nadia Richest man in the world. I've always liked him for one thing.

Oliver What was that?

Nadia I read, before he took a girl on their first date, he insisted she submit to a full medical examination by a doctor of his choosing.

Oliver and Nadia smile.

Now that's what I call romantic.

Oliver Me too.

Nadia Great start to an evening, isn't it?

Oliver And good business for my profession, too.

Nadia Yeah. Yeah, that's what I was thinking.

The two of them stand, amused by each other.

See you later.

Oliver And you.

FIVE

Oliver, alone.

Oliver I used to go to the football when I lived in London. I thought, why's everyone shouting at the referee? He's doing his best. In fact I'm the only fan I know who ever took the referee for a meal. I ran into him as he was leaving the ground – and we fell to talking. I told him I'd liked the way he'd handled things. We went on to a restaurant and I bought him dinner. There's a part of me that likes a well-ordered game.

SIX

The lawn again. The remains of a meal. A CD player is on in the house. Nadia, Philip and Oliver have been eating at a table under the stars. It looks enchanted.

Nadia It seems so long ago, it seems like such a long time ago. I suppose I wasn't there more than eight months . . .

Oliver That's all?

Nadia Probably. But it seems like half a lifetime. When we were in Sarajevo.

There's a moment's silence.

Maybe there was something about my being so young. Most of us were. By the time you've got a family, it's tough, unless your partner's willing to accept you might get a bullet in the throat.

Oliver refers to the scene around them.

Oliver You couldn't sit under the stars. You couldn't eat out?

Nadia You couldn't *eat*. Most nights I was looped, all of us were.

Oliver Looped? What does looped mean?

There is a sudden silence. She looks at him.

Nadia Looped? Looped means drunk.

Everyone is still. Philip watching intently.

You'd go out all day in what we call 'soft skins' . . .

Oliver Say again.

Nadia I thought it would amuse you, that's why I said it.

Oliver All your correspondents' slang.

Nadia Yeah . . .

Oliver You're a tribe.

Nadia Hmm.

Oliver So, 'soft skin'?

Nadia 'Soft skin' meaning a car with no armour. An unarmoured car. A regular car.

Oliver So you went into Shrewsbury today –

Nadia Yeah . . .

Oliver – in a soft skin.

Nadia That's right. Only in Sarajevo you felt it, you really felt it, because you knew there was just a thin layer of tin between you and everything outside. Back at the hotel you were sharing rooms, maybe even sleeping on the floor, you had relationships – these were people you're never going to forget.

Philip looks thoughtful, Oliver notices.

Oliver But you stopped?

Nadia Oh, yes.

Oliver You no longer do it. Why?

Nadia The whole thing. The anger. I found myself addicted.

Oliver Which? To the anger or the way of life?

Nadia Both.

Oliver Anger against what?

Nadia Anger against the world. The world, for standing by, for knowing and not intervening.

Nadia shakes her head, remembering.

Endless days, days lying on a floor in a blackout, watching people die for no purpose, for no reason, except the world's laziness, its fat spoiled sense of itself, its stupid fascination with handbags and losing body weight and who won the Open and who takes an iron to the green. Who cares? Who the fuck cares? The first great war in

Europe since 1945 and nobody's able even to remember which country is which. Which one's Milosevic and which one's the other guy? And which is Croatia, remind me? Is that the one full of Muslims? Or is that Bosnia? I mean, who are we? Who the fuck are we?

There's a moment's silence. Is she drunk? Oliver's gaze is steady.

Three hundred thousand people killed in Europe.

She shakes her head.

There were nights so cold, so pitted from the trace of machine-gun fire, I didn't know concrete could have so many holes and still stand. Like lattice-work. There were bodies – every shape, every colour, bodies rotting in the woods, on building sites – violence, dinning in your head so you wanted to scream. And three hundred miles away there were people going to the opera and hailing gondolas and laughing, not wanting to know, not needing to know. Because they didn't believe the war would come anywhere near them.

Oliver reaches tactfully for the bottle and refills her glass.

Well, now they have their war, and good luck to them.

Oliver You still feel it.

Nadia Yes. I feel it. When I've had a few drinks.

Nadia acknowledges the glass in her hand.

Philip's heard it before.

Philip I don't mind.

Philip smiles a little, reassuring.

Nadia Forgive me. It's a drug. The anger's a drug. I don't like that part of myself.

Oliver You think it's unattractive?

Nadia I don't give a fuck if it's attractive. I only care what it feels like, and it doesn't feel good.

Oliver Because?

Nadia For the obvious reason.

Oliver What's that?

Nadia What, I'm supposed to spend all my time believing that everyone's wrong except me? The world is uncaring and ignorant except for me? Please!

Oliver I understand.

Nadia No, walking around feeling *that* all the time doesn't make anyone happy – unless of course they're a psychopath, or – I don't know – one of your poets.

Nadia stares a moment, the anger unabated.

Oliver And that's the reason you stopped?

Nadia I went out a reporter. I came back an analyst.

Oliver Maybe your temperament was wrong.

Nadia Maybe.

Oliver Psychologically.

Nadia looks up, sharply. Oliver smiles.

To use that word.

Nadia Look, it was simple. It was a simple thing.

Oliver Was it?

Nadia Yes. Don't make it out to be complex. At the end of it all, when I wasn't plain scared or exhausted, I just felt, shit, I'm spending too much of my time feeling self-righteous.

Oliver Why? Why self-righteous?

Nadia Oh look – whatever – half self-righteous, half confused. 'Oh you're a foreign correspondent. How fascinating!' Well, yes, it would be fascinating if anyone took any notice of what we said . . .

Oliver Yes.

Nadia If anyone listened! If anyone did anything because of what we reported!

Oliver waits, tactful.

Oliver But actually you were right. You were right to be angry. Why should you be ashamed? Those people *did* die. And nobody *did* care. Why to apologise?

Nadia looks at him a moment, thoughtful.

Nadia People have forgotten. They've forgotten already. All they think about is terrorism. The truth is there was far more terrorism in the 1980s when nobody thought about it than there is today when nobody thinks about anything else. It's just a fact.

Nadia smiles, relaxing at the irony. She reaches for Philip's hand.

In fact we went – didn't we? – we went to a conference . . .

Oliver Where was this?

Nadia Helsinki.

Philip Helsinki was interesting.

Nadia Philip came.

Philip Just for fun. I was Mr Blye.

Nadia A man got up, very early on, said, 'Nobody in this room is going to die of terrorism. You're more likely to die from swallowing a wasp.'

Philip That's what he said.

Nadia He didn't make himself popular. Not in that company.

They both smile at the memory.

Philip Actually I talked to him later in the bar.

Nadia You did. I remember.

Philip We had a beer. 'The point of a conference,' he said, 'is to be the person who says the stupidest thing.'

Philip smiles, anticipating Nadia.

All right, maybe he didn't say 'stupid' . . .

Nadia Ah well, no . . .

Philip Maybe he said 'provocative'. 'Memorable', I don't know.

Nadia 'Memorable', 'stupid' – there is a difference.

Philip Anyway, we know what he meant. He said, 'That's intellectual life in the West.' He was Egyptian. 'That way you make a reputation,' he said. 'It's a game.'

Nadia is looking disapproving.

It's not what I think, sweet one, it's just what he said.

Nadia laughs, forgiving Philip.

Nadia It's funny. It was a funny weekend to begin with. I made this stupid mistake . . .

Philip I didn't mind.

Nadia I've promised Philip I'll never do it again.

Philip It's just those people. They have no idea.

Oliver Which people?

Nadia I happened to mention to someone what Philip did for a living.

Philip Yeah.

Nadia Well . . .

Philip Who'd have thought so many intellectuals had such bad backs?

Nadia And such a poor idea of how to behave. Not a single one of them didn't sneak up to Philip at some point in the weekend.

Nadia is gathering pace, excited.

People – can I say this?

Philip Sure . . .

Nadia They have this idea of physical therapy as if it were some kind of trade. As if it were plumbing. They treat him as if he's some kind of natural resource.

Philip It's ignorance.

Nadia I'd never met a physical therapist till I met Philip, but even I knew they're not the kind of people you press sweaty bills into their hands. In fact, I tell you, there was one woman there . . .

Philip rolls his eyes.

Philip Oh Jesus!

Nadia Well, it's what happened . . .

Philip Nadia doesn't care for my female clients anyway.

Nadia I don't think that's true. I don't think that's true at all.

Philip Don't you?

Nadia No. As a matter of fact, I don't. And I don't know why you say it. I really don't.

Philip All right, let's say – how do I put this . . .?

Nadia I don't know. How *will* you put this?

Philip All right. At the best of times, Nadia distrusts my female clients of a certain age, of a certain appearance . . .

Nadia Some of them aren't in quite as much pain as they pretend.

It's badinage, but it's spiked. Oliver observes closely.

Philip Anyway, one way or another, this woman's Italian.

Nadia Attractive.

Philip Sort of good-looking. Full-figured.

Nadia Expert on early jihad.

Philip She says, 'Can you possibly just pop up to my room and attend to my grinding discs?'

Philip raises his voice to pre-empt their reaction.

I would like to say, can I just say, this woman is one of the foremost academics in Italy? One of the cleverest women in Italy.

Oliver What did you say?

Philip I said, 'Listen, signora, as a matter of fact, you may not believe this, but in the United States of America, I get two hundred and fifty dollars an hour for what I do. And I deserve it. And anyway I'm on vacation, learning about the pathology of terrorism.'

Oliver What did she say? What did she say to that?

Philip I think she was surprised.

He grins, but Nadia is already continuing.

Nadia I'd already gotten the hang of this fucking woman.

Philip You'd taken against her. Big time.

Nadia Oh, forgive me, but she was one of those self-hating liberals.

Oliver Oh, one of those.

Nadia 'It's our fault. They're right to hate us. If I were them, I'd hate us too.' You know the type.

Oliver I do.

Nadia It's dressed up. It comes all wrapped up in fancy talk, but underneath –

Nadia puts up a hand to forestall him.

Be clear: if what people are saying is that it's our duty to try and understand things from the other point of view, then – believe me – I'm with them. One hundred per cent. But.

Oliver But?

Oliver waits. Nadia doesn't want to spell it out. She sips her wine.

But?

Nadia But that doesn't mean forgetting what we believe in. Does it? We believe in something. We stand for something too. Don't we?

Nadia is appealing directly to Oliver. Philip shrugs.

Philip I don't know. I really don't know. Maybe she just had a bad back.

Nadia Maybe.

Philip The fact is, in America, it's true, I do all sorts of things which aren't strictly medical.

Oliver What sorts of things?

Philip More, well, what people want.

Oliver What they want?

Philip It's not strict medical practice. It's not orthodox medicine.

Oliver What are you saying?

Philip You have to understand: in the States they're really keen about fitness.

Oliver Fitness?

Philip You must know that. Fitness is seen as a vital component of health. That's what my clinics offer.

Oliver Clinics?

Philip Sure.

Oliver I thought you had one. One clinic.

Philip I did. I did have one. Didn't I tell you?

Nadia Now Philip has three.

Oliver Three?

Nadia Three, and counting. He's doing really well.

Nadia grins, provocative. Oliver throws her an uncharitable look.

Philip Anyway, there's a fine line between formal physiotherapy and – I don't know – providing the client with a general sense of well-being.

Oliver What does that mean?

Philip I've just explained what it means.

Oliver It's not strict medical practice, you say. It's not orthodox medicine. Well, then, what is it? What do you offer? Give me an example. Beyond physiotherapy?

Philip All right, I have various people on the staff.

Oliver People? People of what kind?

Philip Therapists, osteopaths . . .

Nadia Personal trainers.

Oliver Jesus Christ, what are you saying, do you send people out for a run?

Philip Dad . . .

Oliver I'm asking. I'm asking a question.

Philip What's so special about running? What's so demeaning about running?

Oliver Do you go running?

Philip No. Not personally. I don't go running. I employ people. Jesus!

Philip turns away, appealing to Nadia.

Didn't I warn you? Isn't this what I said?

Nadia It is, but I don't see why you need to take it so hard.

Nadia grins, enjoying herself.

Oliver Well I must say, if you want to know what I think . . .

Philip I can guess what you think.

Oliver If you want my opinion, I've done a lot of interesting things with my patients, but I've never taken the fuckers out for a jog. I mean, are you serious?

Philip This is a mistake. I should never have raised the subject.

Oliver I'm just saying, putting in all that effort, years of study, education, hard work, and at the end of it all, what are you doing? Handing out those ridiculous little bottles of water and lifting weights?

Philip shakes his head, keeping steady.

Philip Dad. Dad, you know as well as I do that there are cultural factors in medicine. You yourself used to teach me. There is no such thing as pure medicine.

Oliver No. But there is such a thing as charging two hundred and fifty bucks to take obese Americans for a spin in the park.

Philip Do you think that's what I do?

Oliver And there's a word for it too.

Philip Jesus, do you really think that's what I get up to?

Oliver I don't know what you get up to. I'm a doctor, I'm not a personal healer.

Philip They're personal trainers, Dad. Personal *trainers*, not personal healers.

Nadia smiles, having a good time.

Dad, I take on people. Ordinary people. You say, 'Tell them the truth and stay with them to the end.' How about 'delay the end'? That's not ignoble, is it?

Oliver No, it's not.

Philip That's not wrong?

Oliver Certainly not.

Philip 'Put off the end.' Why not? Get fit, feel better, sort out your problems.

Oliver 'Sort out your problems'? God, don't say you talk to the bastards as well!

Philip Isn't it called preventative medicine, Dad, and wasn't it something we were all brought up to believe in?

Oliver Of course.

Philip So?

Philip waits.

So?

Still Oliver says nothing.

We work to stop you getting ill, rather than treating you when it's too late. What's wrong with that? It's the future of medicine, Dad. Or did nobody tell you? Word not reached you? It's all a damned sight more useful than writing prescriptions for a living.

Oliver Don't worry, there's no need to worry about it.

Philip I shan't.

Oliver There's no need to be defensive.

Philip I'm not defensive. I'm aggressive. You're living in the past.

Oliver It's your business. And it's not as if I have such a high opinion of doctors myself.

Nadia Why not? What's that based on?

Oliver I've met a lot of them, remember?

Oliver smiles, convinced.

If you think you're cleverer than your doctor, you're probably right. A degree in medicine is proof of not very much. It's amazing how many people will feel twelve peaches in the supermarket before choosing the one they want, yet they go to the first doctor without a moment's thought. Nothing depending on it, of course, except their life. 'Sorry, Doctor, I didn't want to bother you.' I watch them come through my door: the more modest the manner, the more deadly the disease. Cancer in particular

55

being demonstrably linked to a recent upturn in personal fortune. 'Oh Doctor, I had been through a bad time, but recently I was just beginning to feel better . . .' Wham!

Oliver smiles, at ease.

They look at you all the time as if you could help.

Nadia Can't you?

Oliver Not if they won't help themselves. The first instinct of a sick person is to suspend judgement. Their immediate impulse is very powerful: they want to put themselves in someone else's hands.

Nadia Is that a bad thing?

Oliver When told you're seriously ill, the easiest reaction is to surrender to what you think is authority. When it comes down to it, people would rather gamble than calculate.

Nadia Well, it's an easy mistake to make, isn't it? Doctors are always telling us that they know things which we don't.

Philip Aren't they just?

Oliver I'm a GP, remember? Behind me, the ranks of experts, waiting.

Nadia Did you never want to be an expert yourself?

Oliver I was an expert. Long ago.

There's a silence. They expect him to go on.

Nadia What happened?

Oliver smiles. Then he reaches for the bottle.

Oliver I'm going to give everyone another glass of wine and then we're going to go to bed.

Philip I'm going to take Nadia up Shep Hill.

Oliver Take her up.

Philip waits a moment. Then he gets up, picking up some dishes as he goes.

Philip I need a jumper.

Philip puts a hand on Nadia's shoulder, then goes out.

Nadia What a gorgeous evening.

Oliver Isn't it?

Nadia What time is it?

Oliver Gone twelve.

Nadia He worships you.

Oliver I don't think so.

Nadia Underneath.

Oliver Oh no, not even underneath.

Nadia All right, 'worships' is the wrong word. But he wants to please you.

Oliver Not at all. He wants to get me out of the way.

Nadia Are you sure?

Oliver He wants to forget me. That's why he's here. He's doing his duty. He's not doing anything more. This was never a visit of reconciliation. It's a visit of farewell. I'm enjoying your company, Nadia. But I suspect, whatever happens, I shan't be seeing a lot of you.

Nadia looks at him a moment.

Nadia I'm beginning to see . . . I'm beginning to understand how marked Philip is by his upbringing. He still feels bad he didn't become a doctor.

Oliver Do you think so? I'm not sure. He was going to Newcastle to read medicine but he never took up his place. It was at a difficult time. In the family. He said he'd rather do something less ambitious but do it better. Fair enough. Far less gifted people than Philip saw bones.

Nadia When I met him, in fact, what I liked most was his self-assurance.

Oliver On the surface, Philip has wonderfully high self-confidence and very modest self-esteem. It's a combination you find in all the most winning people.

Nadia Did he inherit that?

Oliver I think you can say: on the contrary. Or not from me, anyway. You might say I've suffered from the opposite. Excessive self-esteem and no self-confidence. Hence.

Nadia Hence? Hence what?

Oliver Hence.

Oliver is thoughtful a moment.

Philip looked after his mother after I left. He's hard-wired. That's what he does best.

Nadia Hard-wired for what?

Oliver No disrespect, but I think you could say he's drawn to difficult women. They've been a constant in his life.

Nadia Until now, you mean?

The two of them are still. It's seductively quiet.

And you?

Oliver Self-evidently, yes. I'm drawn to them too.

Philip appears, silently, tense, behind them. Does Oliver know he's there?

You'll like Shep Hill. The view is extraordinary. By day they say you can see eight counties. And by night, the panoply of the stars. Weather permitting.

Oliver gets up.

If you hear me in the night, don't worry. I like to read. I like to read outside. I'll clear up tomorrow. Leave it for now. Goodnight. Goodnight, son.

This last to Philip as Oliver acknowledges him on his way out. There's a few moments' silence.

Nadia Well?

Philip doesn't answer.

Is something wrong? Do you still want to go for the walk?

Philip Of course I want to go for the walk.

Nadia Well then.

Nadia waits.

I don't understand. Why are you angry?

Philip Because it's an act. It's a mask. You do know that, don't you?

Nadia Does it matter?

Philip He's not who he claims to be.

Nadia You mean underneath?

Nadia smiles at the phrase.

Philip What's funny? Why do you say 'underneath' like that?

Nadia Oh. One of my students – something – anyway, this student kept saying: people are different underneath.

Philip Your student's right.

Nadia waits again.

Nadia What's wrong, Philip?

Philip He sits there so fucking reasonable, as if he were the most reasonable man in the world. He drove my mother nuts. Why do you think she was so unhappy? Anything in a skirt, he fucks it. He's fucked every woman from here to Akaba.

Philip turns towards her.

And he killed one as well. Oh, by accident, it was an accident. But he killed someone.

Nadia A patient?

Philip No. Not a patient.

Nadia Who then?

Philip looks away.

I don't understand. What's up, Philip? This isn't like you.

Suddenly Philip is passionate.

Philip People aren't their views, you know. They aren't their opinions. They aren't just what they say. They aren't the stuff that comes out of their mouths!

Nadia I know that.

Philip Urbane! Civilised! It's a trick. Anyone can do that. It bears no relation to who he is. All that high-mindedness! All that principle! The love of literature!

Philip shakes his head in contempt.

And apart from anything else – I know you won't believe it because it's unbelievable – but he's trying to seduce you.

Nadia Don't be ridiculous. You dope!

Philip He is. He wants to remove his son's girlfriend and take her to bed.

Nadia I don't think so, Philip. I don't think it's likely.

Philip That's what he does. That's the sort of thing he does. Throughout my childhood. He smuggled a French prostitute across the Channel in the boot of a car.

Nadia can't help laughing.

You think it's funny?

Nadia I do think it's funny, yes. For God's sake. You've got to escape this stuff.

Philip Oh yes? Have you escaped this stuff?

Nadia I don't know. I'm searching for any recollection of my father putting hookers in the back of his car.

Philip shakes his head.

And we say trunk. In the States we say trunk.

Philip What about a man who fucks some woman in the living room while my mother's sleeping upstairs?

Nadia Did he do that?

Philip Is that funny? Is that charming?

Nadia concedes.

Nadia All right.

Philip Just look back.

Nadia At what?

Philip At the way the day has gone. Look at it! It began with him undermining. The subtle undermining. Even you must have noticed, the way he set out to subvert you. How he doesn't approve of you going to see the President.

Nadia Oh, that.

Nadia smiles to herself.

Philip How you must have sold out. How you must be some kind of raging opportunist for supporting the war in Iraq. In your own interests, he implied. For reasons of personal ambition, he implied. No integrity, he implied. Well?

Nadia has no answer.

Then calculated – I promise you – calculated, not spontaneous: the switch. Oh, suddenly he doesn't dislike you. Suddenly, he makes you a meal and he thinks you're great. I've seen him do it so many times. So the woman thinks, 'Oh, he's changed towards me. That's interesting. What an interesting man!' God, it's so pathetically obvious. It's Casanova page one.

Nadia Why does it matter?

Philip It matters because it's wrong!

Philip moves away in anger.

And it's disgusting. My whole childhood a trail of women fucked over and spat out while my mother sat alone . . .

There's a silence. Nadia speaks quietly.

Nadia And you don't think now's the time to start to get over it?

Philip Of course I do. I am over it. I got over it. It doesn't matter to me any more. I'm just pointing it out.

Nadia Good.

Philip What does 'good' mean?

Nadia What do you think it means?

Nadia waits a moment, taking him seriously. She's calm.

Where's your sense of humour? Don't say you've lost it.

Philip I haven't lost it. I've mislaid it. I'll find it again.

Nadia When? When will you find it?

Philip Soon. I'll find it soon.

Nadia smiles.

Nadia Philip, we came for a vacation. We came as a couple. I want us to leave as a couple.

Philip Yes, well, that would be the definition of a successful weekend.

Nadia I've been honest with you. I've been in a series of relationships which didn't work. One reason: I was often with volatile men. I told you that. You're not like that. Let's say, after some of my experiences, it was a very attractive quality.

Philip Was?

Nadia Is. It is a very attractive quality.

There's a moment's silence. Philip speaks without bitterness.

Philip Too difficult for you? Too much trouble for you? This whole thing too much trouble for the veteran of Sarajevo?

Nadia Just, I don't like to see people suffer over things they can do nothing about.

Philip I thought those were the things in life we *have* to suffer about.

Nadia I hope not. I really do hope not.

Philip smiles, conceding.

So. Tell me. What are we going to do on that hill?

Philip What would you like to do on that hill?

Nadia Good.

The argument is resolved. They stand in each other's arms.

End of Act One.

Act Two

SEVEN

Philip, alone.

Philip Asleep. Fast asleep. And dreaming of childhood. My father, the famous physician. The memory of my mother, sitting on the side of the bed, her hair tumbling over her face. Me, alone in my room, looking up at the sound of her crying, as if the plane to America were already waiting, one day, many years later, to take me away . . .

EIGHT

The middle of the night. The lawn. Oliver is sitting in a dressing gown on one of the canvas chairs, reading, a small battery-powered light attached to the book. He does not hear as Nadia comes, sleepy, barefoot, from the direction of the house. She approaches, and he turns.

Oliver Do you know what Richard Nixon said when they took him to the Great Wall of China?

Nadia No. No, what did Nixon say?

Oliver He said, 'This is a great wall.'

Nadia smiles.

It's awesome, isn't it?

Nadia Kind of.

Oliver What I admire: it's majestic in its simplicity. Of all the reactions a human being could have on being shown a wall, Nixon's is the purest. The most undeniable.

Nadia Nobody fools Richard Nixon.

Oliver Quite.

Nadia He knows a great wall when he sees one.

Oliver I think it may just be the all-time Zen remark of politics.

Nadia moves forward to look at the stars.

Nadia What a night! My God, what a night!

Oliver It's beautiful here, isn't it?

Nadia It's very beautiful.

Oliver Aren't I lucky?

Oliver smiles to himself.

I don't think my son will be very happy to wake and find you gone.

Nadia He won't wake up. He sleeps like a log.

Oliver Not you?

Nadia doesn't answer.

Nadia Did you cook the supper yourself?

Oliver Who else?

Nadia Single-handed?

Oliver Did you think I bought it in?

Nadia How did you do the salad? It was delicious.

Oliver Pomegranate seeds. It's a trick. It's a cheap trick.

Nadia is looking out at the night. Oliver puts his book aside.

Politicians only speak to please. Or to pre-empt an argument. Or to fill an uncomfortable silence. 'This is a great wall.' How can you teach that?

Nadia I'm interested in the art of settling differences. To me, that's what it's about. How do we all get along when we want different things?

Oliver Is that what it's about?

Nadia I think it is.

Oliver Nothing nobler than that? Nothing more heroic?

Nadia There are twice as many people in the world as there were twenty years ago. As more people live closer, their differences become more intense. For the Vietnam peace talks, two months were spent simply deciding the arrangement of the table. The war in Yugoslavia – that took years to resolve. At the end, there was a twenty-day session in the Bob Hope Conference Center in Dayton, Ohio. I was there. It needs determination. It needs resolve. And a measure of honesty. The good people are the negotiators. The bad people are the posturers.

Oliver That's the secret, is it? Sitting at the table? Staying at the table? Not leaving?

Nadia looks at him a moment. Then she shrugs.

Nadia Look, I understand the urge people have to turn their backs. Many of us, after all, escaped from Europe . . .

Oliver Your own family?

Nadia My great-grandparents.

Oliver Where to?

Nadia Northern California.

Oliver Ah . . .

Nadia I come from a liberal background.

Oliver I guessed.

Nadia Like your own, I assume. The way you think, the way you speak, they're familiar to me. Public service, public ethics.

Oliver Are your parents still alive?

Nadia Why, yes.

Oliver Together?

Nadia shakes her head.

Nadia Anyway – whatever – our first instinct as immigrants was to remove ourselves from your disputatious continent.

Oliver Fair enough.

Nadia That's why we went.

Oliver You were right.

Nadia To get away.

Oliver Who can blame you?

Nadia And if you look at recent American history – World War Two, Korea, Vietnam, the Cold War – then it's hardly surprising, is it, that so many of us are happier within our own borders? What's the point of being rich if you can't enjoy your wealth? When the Soviet Union collapsed, there was to be a dividend. We would live our own lives. But the opposite has happened. We're more and more drawn into the world.

Oliver smiles.

Oliver You weren't exactly drawn into it, were you?

Nadia Well . . .

Oliver More like, you stepped into it, don't you think?

Nadia Depends which part.

Oliver Barged in, I'd say. The West's been using Islam as a useful enemy for as long as anyone can remember. 'Shall we go to Constantinople and take the Turk by the beard? Shall we not?' It's from *Henry V*.

There is a silence. Oliver speaks quietly.

Your feet will get wet. The dew comes early.

Oliver's tone is so private that Nadia turns.

Nadia And you? You read all night?

Oliver I don't need much sleep. It's a doctor's trick. Snatching sleep on the wards.

Nadia Everything's a trick to you. You use that word all the time.

Oliver Do I?

Nadia Yes.

Nadia stands, not moving.

Oliver How was the hill?

Nadia I'm sorry?

Oliver Didn't you go up Shep Hill?

Nadia Oh yes. It was spectacular.

Oliver What did you do up there?

Nadia hesitates for only a second.

I'm sorry. What a stupid question.

Nadia And the view was great.

Oliver It is. It always is.

There's a moment's silence.

Nadia Philip . . . Philip began to tell me about his mother.

Oliver Did he?

Nadia He began to open up. He talks very little about her.

Oliver Maybe there's a reason.

Nadia catches his tone.

Nadia It was a bad separation?

Oliver You could say.

Nadia He said agonising.

Oliver It was.

Nadia She lives in North London? In your old house?

Oliver Yes.

Nadia She never left?

Oliver shakes his head.

Oliver Long before I decided to go, there were problems. She'd become obsessed with a need for control. To control life.

Nadia Her own life?

Oliver Certainly. And, by extension, the lives of others.

Nadia She's a doctor too?

Oliver nods.

What do you mean by 'control'?

Oliver It took different forms. It's one thing to put a label on the sugar jar saying 'Sugar'. You can put the word 'Tea' on the jar where you keep the tea. But when you type the word 'Fridge' and put it on the fridge, then the signs are that you're in a certain amount of trouble. Easiest to say, her world shrank. From being a woman in the world she became a woman in flight from it. Even the trip to the hospital became unbearable to her.

Nadia Because?

Oliver Oh, the feeling of being seen.

Nadia waits.

The feeling of being watched.

Nadia Was she watched?

Oliver Of course not. Nobody gave a damn.

Nadia Maybe that was the problem?

Oliver I don't think so.

Nadia The feeling of being neglected. Your absences.

Oliver thinks a moment.

Oliver Look, you know, plainly it's clear –

Nadia All right, I shouldn't have said that –

Oliver Say what you like.

Nadia It's none of my business.

Oliver Philip has his own view of things, of course he does. His mother's mental state is an issue between us. She's been on medication for a number of years. Philip thinks I'm to blame.

Nadia He didn't actually say that.

Oliver Didn't he? It's no secret. Philip disapproved. Philip disapproved of our marriage. Of the kind of marriage we had.

Nadia What kind of marriage was that?

Oliver The open kind. The kind in which love is free.

There is a silence. Nadia says nothing.

Philip's also in flight.

Nadia Flight from what?

Oliver Why, from me. Why did he go to live in America?

Nadia He's never said that.

Oliver No, but you know Philip. It's obvious. Philip defined his life in opposition to mine. England. America. Many partners. One. Pleasure in discourse. Pleasure in silence. I like early Dylan. He prefers late. That's who he is. See it as a kind of strength. He's an interesting chap.

Oliver shrugs slightly.

For as long as he could, he tried to keep the peace between me and his mother. Then at a certain point he was forced to choose. I don't hold it against him. He likes me but he'll never trust me. Who's to say he's wrong?

They look at each other for a moment, level.

Nadia Please. I'm not taking sides. I'm simply asking.

Oliver It's fine.

Nadia I wouldn't have raised the subject, but after all.

Oliver After all?

Nadia We're alone on the lawn. There's no one around.

Oliver smiles.

Oliver It was you who said you needed private things to stay private.

Nadia I did.

Oliver So? What is it? The night? The night is changing you?

There's a moment. Nadia looks at him.

Nadia In combat medicine, there's this moment – after a disaster, after a shooting – there's this moment, the vertical hour, when you can actually be of some use.

Oliver Of use to me?

Oliver looks, disbelieving. Then he begins to speak decisively.

Very well. Our marriage. If you want to know. If you're interested.

Nadia I am.

Oliver I've tried to understand. I've tried to understand what happened between us. Pauline began to suffer from the very thing she most wanted.

Nadia What was that thing?

Oliver Freedom. She suffered from freedom.

There's a moment. Oliver waits.

Pauline said to me, very early on, she said, I remember her saying: 'I don't believe human beings need to practise holding on. Holding on is easy. It's letting go we need to learn.'

Nadia Really?

Oliver Yes.

Nadia That's a hard view.

Oliver Is it?

Nadia Certainly.

Oliver I don't think so.

Nadia It's a hard way to live.

Oliver Excuse me, but I'm not sure anyone who makes their living as a foreign correspondent is in any position to judge.

Nadia Why not?

Oliver What, rushing abroad to dangerous places?

Nadia It isn't that simple.

Oliver Isn't it?

Nadia Are you telling me I was running away?

Oliver I didn't say that.

Nadia Well what?

Oliver All I'm saying: you didn't choose the most obvious way of life for someone who wants to invest everything in another human being.

Nadia Maybe, but I gave it up, remember?

He looks a moment, but Nadia doesn't go on.

Oliver All right. So. Pauline arrived in my bed with no intention of staying there. We were carefree. We worked day and night.

Nadia You worked in a hospital?

Oliver Yes.

Nadia That's when you were a specialist?

Oliver Training. Training to be. Pauline was already living in a certain way – we were medical students, we grew up in the sixties. For God's sake, the body's our field. If you've ever worried what a doctor is thinking when he asks you to take your clothes off, you needn't worry any more. I can tell you the answer. Never underestimate the medical professional's capacity for filthy-mindedness. Pauline had no intention of changing

74

just because she'd met me. You may not believe this, but people of that age, we had an idea. Underneath all the bullshit, all the evasion, all the 'I'll see you tomorrow' when you mean *you won't – ever* – you'd cross the road if you so much as saw the other person coming – we actually had an idea.

Nadia What kind of idea?

Oliver We believed.

Nadia What did you believe?

Oliver Oh. The more people you sleep with, the more you learn.

There's a silence. Oliver is quiet.

The liberation of Eros. All right, it's no longer a fashionable point of view.

Nadia You could say.

Oliver It went the way of smoking. But that's what we thought. The more widely you love, the wider your capacity for love becomes.

Nadia Did you really believe that?

Oliver It was a different time.

Nadia It certainly was.

Oliver Love's a feeling, isn't it? It's a feeling. It isn't the truth.

Nadia Is it?

There's a silence.

Go on.

Oliver There was a lot of talk about ownership. About not being owned. People not being property. William

Blake to his wife: 'If you wish my happiness, how can you not wish me happy with someone else?'

Nadia grins.

Nadia They're handy, these poets of yours, aren't they?

Oliver Well, they are.

Nadia Never really on your own, are you?

Oliver Not really.

Nadia You always have a poet around.

Nadia shakes her head, disbelieving.

I must say, it does take a particular gift, it takes a particular flair – you sleep with a lot of women and somehow you want to claim it *means* something?

Oliver Well?

Nadia I have to ask, this 'generation' you talk about – you think it was time well spent, do you, dreaming up a philosophy to justify what anyone else would have known was simple selfishness?

Oliver I think it may go a little deeper than that.

Nadia Do you? What's the idea? You sleep with a lot of people and it's an *ideal*?

Oliver Well, so it was.

Nadia I mean, the obvious question, why not just fuck 'em for fun?

Oliver All right . . .

Nadia That's what the rest of us do.

There is a moment's silence.

Did do. Did do.

Oliver Before you met Philip.

Nadia Right.

Nadia smiles, acknowledging the slip. She makes a gesture of 'What can you do?'

Oliver You may be right. Though it didn't feel like that at the time. For a start, we were a lot happier than our parents.

Nadia Isn't everyone?

Oliver smiles, acknowledging the truth.

Oliver As time went by, I admit, there was a burden of guilt.

Nadia Specifically?

Oliver The ending of the relationship was, for one reason or another, spectacular. Has Philip never said?

Nadia shakes her head.

But also the more general question: could I have made this woman less unhappy?

Nadia Could you?

Oliver How can you tell? I'm nearly sixty.

Nadia Does that make a difference?

Oliver I've learnt a little respect for mystery.

Oliver smiles.

The fashion now is to attack Freud. He's not acceptable, is he?

Nadia Freud?

Oliver Not any more.

Nadia I don't know. Isn't he?

Oliver But there he is, working away, trying to define the impossible line between what we need to suffer and what we don't. We can try to understand each other, we have to, it's our life's work, but finally Freud comes to us and reports that people remain unknowable. It's strange, isn't it? It's typical that we're all so keen to dismiss this man – 'a prisoner of his time', we say – but in their resentment, their determination he should be obsolete, nobody sees, nobody remembers: there's something beautiful about what Freud's telling us. So many scientists leave the world diminished. He leaves it enlarged. He doesn't explain life. Rather he warns us to take care because so much is inexplicable.

Oliver smiles.

Nadia Is that his message?

Oliver Among others.

Nadia I've never really known.

Oliver You don't approve?

Nadia Not that. More: one of my students –

Oliver Yes?

Nadia – brought Freud up, only the other day.

Oliver And?

Nadia And I did notice, it did occur to me, people usually talk about Freud when they want to get their own way. They talk about Freud because they don't like the look of the facts.

Oliver You mean they use him because he's convenient?

Nadia Exactly. That's exactly what I mean.

Oliver In what way?

Nadia 'I don't want to fuck you.' 'Oh yes you do. *Underneath.*'

They both smile.

Freud's used to justify everything, isn't he? 'It's not my fault. It was my mother.' Hear the word 'Freud' and it's like a flag. You know there's an excuse coming. I mean, wouldn't it be refreshing to restore the notion of *bad behaviour*? And people being responsible for what they do? You do something wrong, you own up, you pay the price! Wouldn't that be refreshing?

Oliver Goodness.

Nadia I know.

Oliver Well, goodness.

Oliver smiles. Nadia stands, slightly taken aback by her own outburst.

Something tells me you're winding up for a drink.

Nadia As a matter of fact, I am. Do you mind?

Oliver Not in the slightest.

Nadia What time is it?

Oliver Five.

Nadia OK.

Oliver Five's a good time for a Chardonnay.

Nadia pours a huge slug from a remaining bottle.

Nadia I'm sorry . . .

Oliver No . . .

Nadia It's ridiculous.

Oliver Not at all.

Nadia I know I sound harsh . . .

Oliver It doesn't bother me. Nothing bothers me.

Nadia But I travel in so many countries where all this stuff counts for nothing.

Oliver I'm sure.

Nadia It counts for nothing! It means nothing!

Nadia has raised her voice, vehement. Oliver throws an anxious glance to the house.

I don't know, you can't help noticing when you return . . . when I came back, last time, say, from Iraq . . .

Oliver Is that when you met Philip?

Nadia Yes.

Oliver How long ago?

Nadia A year. It was a year ago.

Nadia stands a moment, thinking.

What is it now? Seventy-nine journalists already dead, the most dangerous war in the history of my profession.

Oliver Your ex-profession.

Nadia OK. Anyway, this last time I went to observe, not to report. I went as an academic. Not that it matters. They kill you whoever you are. And yes, it's true, I came back to my nice job at Yale, I looked at these kids, looked at my colleagues, and I thought, 'I know I've got to resist this feeling, I know I've got to fight it, but these people seem spoiled. They seem soft and spoiled.'

Nadia thinks, then drinks her wine.

Oliver And so we are.

Nadia As if nothing worried them except their jobs and their bosses and their fucking love lives. And I remember thinking, 'I have no right to despise these people, I have no right to look down on them . . .'

Oliver Nor have you.

Nadia I remember thinking, 'I don't like this feeling. I don't like this feeling at all. I'm not different. I'm the same. I'm not better. Just as confused. Just as lost. Covering up by always having a purpose, always having an intention . . .'

Oliver But underneath?

Nadia Exactly.

There is a long silence. Nadia shakes her head.

'Underneath.'

Suddenly Nadia's eyes well up with tears. She stands, fighting them back. With no warning at all, she is crying. Oliver makes the slightest move towards her, but she puts up a hand. Then she goes and pours herself a second, large glass of wine.

Oliver So?

Nadia So – something I've never done – I went to the gym.

Oliver Well, fair enough.

Nadia The classic response – go to the gym, make minute adjustments to the proportion of body fat to muscle, conform to social norms. Skinny! Skinny! I was in the gym. I was standing there, thinking nothing, or rather just thinking, 'Live a long life! Look as much like other people as possible!' And suddenly there was Philip. Standing near me. Incredibly composed. Strong.

Oliver What did you think?

Nadia I thought, 'Here's someone who looks as if he knows who he is.'

Nadia shakes her head.

Shaming.

Oliver Why? Why shaming?

Nadia I suppose . . . I'm ashamed to say this. I'm not sixteen.

Oliver It was romantic?

Nadia Kind of. Yes.

Oliver Say it.

Nadia You're not supposed to like men's looks, are you? Aren't looks meant to be a sign of shallowness? They say, 'He was good-looking, in a shallow sort of way.' They never say, 'He was good-looking and it was profound.' They never say that.

Nadia shrugs.

Oh, be clear, it wasn't just his looks . . .

Oliver Of course not.

Nadia For a start, I liked the idea that he didn't come from my world.

Oliver Well, no.

Nadia He's not bothered by things that bother me. Nothing he couldn't do. Fix a car. My car broke down. Even my roof. He knew what store to go to, he could re-tile a roof. There he was, within hours of our meeting.

Oliver Up on your roof?

Nadia I remember thinking, 'I've never met a man like this. A man who can actually do things.' I wanted him.

Oliver looks at her thoughtfully.

I'd always associated passion with turbulence. With upset. This was passion, only benign. That's rare. That's very rare.

Oliver I imagine, after what you'd been through, it came as a relief.

Nadia It did.

Oliver I'm sure.

Nadia I might as well tell you, there are so many kinds of men who don't attract me. Include in that: journalists, academics, people who talk about politics all day.

Oliver You mean, people like you?

Nadia Exactly. I've never been attracted to anyone like me.

They both smile.

Oliver So who does attract you?

Nadia Oh . . .

Oliver You have the air of someone who's had their heart broken.

Nadia What makes you say that? Why do you say that?

Oliver looks at her, not answering.

Out of the blue, out of the blue, you say that.

Nadia looks shaken. She stands, waiting for him to explain.

Oliver All right. Last night, when you were talking, when you were talking about your past, about Sarajevo, I couldn't help thinking: this is a woman who's been badly hurt.

Nadia What, you think you can see right through me?

Oliver No.

Nadia Though, of course, it's not surprising, is it, given your area of expertise? All your background, all your experience . . .

Oliver All right . . .

Nadia All your women.

The mood has changed. Nadia is on the attack.

In fact, would you mind, can I just say something?

Oliver Of course.

Nadia Earlier . . .

Oliver Yes?

Nadia When you were telling me about your marriage? How difficult it was. How hard to understand. I found myself wondering. You were speaking so tenderly. With such longing. OK, it must be tempting, but weren't you rather overdoing the clouds of romantic mystery?

Oliver Was I?

Nadia It's one of those things. One of those gender things. Women's ears tend to get fine-tuned.

Oliver Fine-tuned? Fine-tuned to what?

Nadia Lying. Men who lie.

Nadia looks, unapologetic.

You made a deal. Didn't you? Isn't that the truth? The two of you made a cynical deal. It suited you. As time went by, it turned out it didn't suit her. She grew out of it. You didn't. Are things really any more complicated than that?

For the first time she has reached Oliver. Nadia looks at him, then almost laughs before she moves away. He speaks quietly, to himself.

Oliver I think they are. I don't think that begins to get near it.

Nadia In fact, I can't believe it, I sat here yesterday, I was sitting here . . .

Oliver So?

Nadia Eating my breakfast, you made me feel terrible, you gave me shit about going to see my President . . .

Oliver What shit? I don't remember giving you shit.

Nadia As if you could judge me! As if somehow you were entitled to judge me!

Again, Nadia has raised her voice, newly confident of what she wants to say.

The funny thing is, I didn't even mind at the time.

Oliver Didn't mind what?

Nadia My interrogation.

Oliver Oh come on! Interrogation!

Nadia I didn't even notice. At the time I just thought, 'Oh this is an Englishman. I've heard about this, this is the kind of guy who sits on his lawn and thinks it's demeaning to get involved in anything.'

Oliver Is that me? Is that mean to be a description of me?

Nadia Charming as hell. But lethal.

Nadia looks at him a moment.

If you really want to know, I didn't go to the White House because I was under any illusions.

Oliver Of course not.

Nadia I wasn't going for myself. I went because I thought it was necessary.

Oliver Sure.

Nadia I went because I thought it might be useful. It might be worthwhile.

Oliver I'm sure. I'm sure you did.

Nadia waits.

Nadia Well? What's wrong with that?

Oliver I didn't say it was wrong.

Nadia What's the alternative? We just give up, do we?

Oliver Of course not.

Nadia The rest of us give up?

Oliver says nothing.

It's easy, isn't it? It's easy, your position?

Oliver Do I have a position?

Nadia Stay home, sit on your hands, look superior, say this administration's nothing but a bunch of seedy opportunists and crooks?

Oliver You said it.

Nadia Yes, but like it or not, they're the party in power.

Oliver Of course.

Nadia They're the guys.

Oliver Of course.

Nadia And what do we do about the fact that on this one occasion they happened to be right? Whoever they are. Fuck their ideology, fuck their golf-cart morals and their tenth-rate business deals – but I happen to agree with them on one basic thing: it isn't a bad idea when people are suffering – when you're faced with that scale of suffering, you act. You help.

Again, Nadia has raised her voice. Oliver looks again to the house.

Oliver All right, no need to jump off a building.

Nadia I'm not.

Oliver Defensive or what?

Nadia Oh, we're all defensive, aren't we? Don't we both have things to be defensive about?

Oliver just looks at her, a little shaken.

Yeah, sure, you're the generation that talked about ideals, have I got that right?

Oliver Roughly.

Nadia Everything had to be an ideal.

Oliver So?

Nadia Everything was a matter of principle! You may have noticed – we are more practical. I admire the practical people. I deal with what's there.

Nadia nods, bitter, speaking from the heart.

'Ancient hatreds', that's what they always tell you. In the Balkans I got so tired of hearing that phrase. 'Ancient hatreds'. Whenever people tried to explain what the hell was going on. Oh yes, people love ancient hatreds, because if it's an ancient hatred, what can you do? You don't have to do anything. They tell you all the time in Israel, in Palestine, in Bosnia, in Chechnya, in Ireland, 'Oh there's nothing you can do until these crazy people decide to stop killing each other. They *like* killing each other.' Well it's never true. What is true is that wherever there's a history of violence you can be sure to find unscrupulous politicians looking to exploit it. But underneath there are always rational causes. And 'ancient hatreds' is just the phrase they drag out when they can't be bothered to do anything at all.

Nadia looks at Oliver.

It's taken America years, you could say it's taken us centuries to understand that we have responsibilities. This was an isolationist government, refusing to do anything that wasn't grubbing for votes and making money. Do you think I haven't paid my price on campus? Kids with four-by-fours and private trust funds, coming in Gucci jeans and designer T-shirts saying, 'Oh it's a matter of principle. I won't take class with Nadia Blye.'

Oliver Has that really happened?

Nadia Nobody wanted to listen, nobody wanted to hear. I could have been in foxholes, I could have been shot at by every insurgent on earth – and kids would still come snarling up to me: 'Hey, didn't you go to the White House? Aren't you the woman who spoke to George Bush?'

Nadia impulsively moves away.

What do you think? What do you think it was like? That day I went to Washington . . .

Oliver I can't imagine.

Nadia It's true, I walked in that day, I thought this is the oddest thing I've ever done in my life.

Oliver I'm sure.

Nadia Who are these people? What am I doing here? And then you remember it's democracy you're there to defend. Yeah. Freedom. So. In fact, when it comes down to it, there's only one 'principle'. I'll tell you what that principle is: push up your sleeves, put away your personality and get on with the work.

Nadia is quieter now, her emotion raw.

The only reason you're there, the reason you're talking to the President, is that you happen to be an expert on issues exactly like this. And isn't it better to talk to people we have nothing in common with? Isn't that better? Isn't that more useful than just talking to ourselves?

Oliver Yes.

Oliver smiles.

Yes, by all means. It's better. Always assuming people are listening.

Nadia Of course.

Oliver It's quite a large assumption. Isn't it?

Nadia just looks at him. She is apprehensive now, nervous.

And you have to consider another possibility, don't you?

Nadia What's that? What other possibility?

Oliver It must have occurred to you, I would have thought: don't you have to take care you're not being used?

Nadia is quiet, no longer fighting him.

Nadia Yes. Of course. I accept that. I know that. Of course I do.

Oliver shrugs slightly.

Oliver After all, I don't know what you told the President.

Nadia No, you don't.

Oliver I wasn't there.

Nadia No, you weren't.

Oliver I can only guess. I assume it wasn't you who said, 'Do it regardless of whether it's legal.' I assume you didn't say, 'Drop bombs where you like. Don't take field hospitals, lawyers, sanitary engineers, doctors, or any of the apparatus that any decent resultant society might actually need. Forget those. Don't take enough troops. Just bomb and hope for the best.' I can't see you saying that.

Oliver waits a moment. It is now very quiet.

I assume you didn't say, 'Be sure to have no plan for civil society. Take no notice of international opinion. Manufacture intelligence from the most corrupt and dishonest elements in the country. Sanction torture. Ignore objections. Be deaf to criticism. Somehow magically order will come out of chaos.'

Nadia No. You're right. I didn't say that.

Oliver You didn't say, 'It doesn't matter if tens of thousands of people get killed, just so long as they're not Americans . . .'

They both are still, Nadia conceding at last.

Nadia Jesus, what a mess.

Oliver You could say.

Nadia We certainly made a mess of it, didn't we? Oh God, I'm so tired.

Nadia is vulnerable. There are tears in her eyes again.

It's so much easier to do nothing than something.

Oliver reaches out a hand. She takes it. There is a silence, he seated, she standing, holding hands. Then, after a while, Nadia shakes her head, and goes and sits down at the abandoned dinner table.

It's true. As you guessed.

Oliver What's true?

Nadia I did have a relationship.

Oliver doesn't move.

I did. A journalist. He's Polish. I'd been with him in the Balkans. Then, as luck would have it, who's the first person I meet when I drive into Baghdad? What you might call a hard-line reporter. Meaning: fair chance he's going to get killed. Meaning also: he doesn't give a fuck about anything. As it turns out, including himself.

Oliver That's difficult.

Nadia It is. Or anyone else. Including me.

Nadia thinks a moment.

Six foot tall. Thin as a rake. A professional. Meaning: he has no opinions. Opinions are for idiots, he says. Oh, he gets angry. He gets involved. But it's the job he loves. Dodging bullets. He's unequivocal. He says he couldn't live in the West.

Oliver What you're saying is, he's heroic.

Nadia Yes. Heroic. Heroic. Completely oblivious of his own personal safety. And in the evening . . . he likes to get drunk.

Oliver What's his name?

Nadia Marek.

Nadia looks away.

I couldn't take it. He turned me inside out. Like gutting a fish. I'd never known anything like it. I was jealous. Oh, not just ordinary jealous. But wanting to be as alive as he was. So little frightened. I thought: I can't do anything. I can't work, I can't sleep. This will kill me.

Nadia shakes her head slightly.

Anyway, I came back to America. I met Philip. You'll think me contemptible.

Oliver No.

Nadia I want to tell you something. I shouldn't. You're going to hate me for saying this.

Oliver Please.

Nadia I thought: if I just live quietly with Philip, then I'll get my private life out of the way.

Oliver sits back, as if this is what he's been waiting for.

And that's what happened.

Oliver I see.

Nadia It's been very peaceful. I've been at peace. I've gotten on with my work.

Oliver That's good.

Nadia The students don't bother me. The stuff on campus – it doesn't touch me.

Oliver Good.

Nadia Why should it? Philip's always there. He's there when I need him.

Oliver Does he know?

Nadia Oh yes.

Oliver About who came before him?

Nadia Certainly.

Oliver He doesn't mind?

Nadia doesn't answer.

What I'm asking: he can live with the difference?

Nadia looks at Oliver sharply.

Nadia He's not second best. If that's what you mean.

Oliver I didn't mean that.

Nadia Good. He's different. Easier.

Oliver And easier's better?

Nadia hesitates.

Nadia I thought so. Yes. I had thought so. Until I came here.

Nadia shakes her head.

Oliver Are you all right?

Nadia I'm fine.

Oliver Too much to drink perhaps?

Nadia No. Too little.

They both smile.

What about you?

Oliver I'm not drinking.

Nadia No. That's not what I meant.

Oliver now understands her.

Oliver Oh. Oh I see.

Nadia I've told you what happened to me.

Oliver Yes.

Nadia Well?

Oliver It's so long since I talked about anything. To anyone.

Nadia Exactly.

He looks at her for a while, then concedes.

Oliver All right.

Nadia Are you going to tell me about the person you killed?

Oliver Yes. That person. It's what ended my marriage. It was an accident.

Nadia I hadn't imagined you killed someone deliberately.

Oliver No.

Oliver hesitates.

Nadia Tell me.

Oliver Well, you have to understand, I don't know if you know this, the guts are distributed between various specialists. I was a nephrologist. I was very much the man. The man you went to, in that ridiculous snobbish way people have. 'Who's best? Who's best for kidneys?' 'Oliver Lucas for kidneys.' I was very, very rich and conceited. Arrogant, in the way doctors are. I'd been in the country. East Anglia. I was driving back.

Nadia Had you been drinking?

Oliver No. I'd spent an afternoon in bed with a friend. I left about five. I thought, if I can be home by supper I can avoid the inevitable scene. I was on a country road. The man was in his mid-eighties, in one of those – I don't know, we have them in England – Eastern European cars, incredibly lightweight. Not even soft skins, no skins.

He went straight into me. He never even saw me. I'd signalled incorrectly.

Oliver looks straight at her.

The police afterwards said it would have made no difference. It was what they call a fifty-fifty. Yes, I'd signalled left, intending to go right, but this man was on the wrong side of the road.

Oliver stops a moment, thoughtful.

You might say, all right, he was going to die anyway . . .

Nadia He was in his eighties.

Oliver That's right. Sometimes at the hospital it used to occur to us we were slaving to save a human being who'd be dead in two weeks. But that's the contract.

Nadia What's the contract?

Oliver Life at all costs.

Oliver looks at Nadia, apparently casual.

I also killed the woman.

Nadia What?

Oliver Yes. She died at my side. In the crash. I was giving her a lift back to London.

There is a silence.

Nadia I see.

Oliver She was killed instantly. We spun over and I laid her out in the road. Bad luck. She hit her head at an unlucky angle. Very little visible damage. She had a silk scarf round her neck. Soaked in blood. Very shocking. Apart from that, nothing.

Nadia Who was she?

Oliver I'd met her at a party. You might say, I didn't even know her. But of course I did know her. We'd spent several afternoons together. But I didn't . . . Oh God, it turned out she'd told me all sorts of lies. Almost nothing she'd told me was true. She was a fantasist. She was married. Something she'd omitted to mention. Not that I'd asked. That wasn't the nature of the venture. But still.

Nadia is shocked, silent.

Nadia My God.

Oliver Exactly. From the bed to the roadside.

Nadia How old was she?

Oliver Young. Younger than me. There was a husband, who was . . . lunatic. Impossible. Understandably. Wanted to sue me. A lot of stuff about the General Medical Council. But it was an accident. After all, in theory, I'd done nothing wrong.

Oliver is lost in thought.

It was Marx, I think, who said that shame is the only revolutionary emotion. And so. I gave her everything.

Nadia Pauline?

Oliver I gave her the house and every penny I had.

Nadia You left your practice?

Oliver I did.

Nadia And came here?

Oliver I left London. I came to live in Shropshire. I moved away to where I wouldn't do harm.

Oliver shrugs slightly.

Of course for Pauline – for Philip also – it was a simple issue. My wife had always said I was a despicable person.

So at last here was the proof. She detected the workings of justice. It was what I deserved. For myself I was tired of justifying myself to another human being. I walked out. I came here to be a GP. It felt clean, it felt refreshing to stand aside from the racket. I need enough money to live, to drink decent wine, to buy books. Why do I need money to put in the bank?

Oliver is quiet now.

To me, you see, the lesson was different. It wasn't what Philip believes. To me the lesson was: you can't spend your life in flight. Sometime you have to stop running.

Oliver looks at her.

I'm sorry. Perhaps I shouldn't have said that.

Nadia No. No. You must say what you like.

Oliver I see life for what it is: fragile. Every moment for what it is: potentially disastrous. And, at all times, I try to take care.

Philip appears silently behind them, in night clothes. He is very quiet.

Philip Here you are.

Nadia Yes. I was talking to your father.

Philip I can see. I was dreaming. I dreamt you weren't beside me. Then I woke up.

Nadia Philip . . .

Philip It's all right.

Nadia We were just talking.

Philip What else would you be doing? What time is it?

Oliver It isn't yet six.

Philip moves barefoot across the lawn, the two of them watching.

Philip It's a beautiful morning.

Oliver It is.

Philip Of course that's what you don't get in America.

Oliver What's that?

Philip The softness. The softness of the dawn. Nadia's an early riser. So she's already at work when I wake. I look out the window for a moment. It's the only time of day when I do feel nostalgic.

There is a silence, no one daring to speak.

Oliver Then what happens?

Philip Oh. I go to make coffee and I cheer up.

Philip turns.

I'll make some now. Do we all want coffee?

Oliver I'll make it. I can make it.

Oliver's beeper sounds.

Nadia What's that?

Oliver It's probably a customer. I'm on death watch. A patient of mine. I may have to go anyway. Excuse me.

Oliver has got up. He goes out, taking some dirty dishes with him.

Nadia Are you angry?

Philip Why should I be angry?

Nadia Then good.

There is another silence.

He hasn't said one single word in any way disloyal to you.

Philip Of course not. He's not stupid.

Nadia What does that mean?

Philip He has a strategy.

Philip shakes his head slightly.

I knew you'd get up. I didn't need to look. I knew you'd go to him.

Nadia Were you awake?

Philip doesn't answer.

And as it happens, I wasn't looking for him. It never occurred to me. I simply had jet lag. I didn't even know he was outside.

Philip Didn't you?

Nadia What's wrong? What's wrong with our talking?

Philip Because I'm sure he was spinning a line.

Nadia That's not fair.

Philip Isn't it? And tell me, how would you know?

There's a silence.

Nadia Talk to me, Philip. You use these silences. You use them against me. Tell me what's wrong.

Philip turns and looks at her.

Philip He wants you to leave me. I know him. That's what he wants. He wants to split us up.

Nadia Why would he want that?

Philip He's jealous.

Nadia Why is he jealous?

Philip Isn't it obvious?

Nadia Tell me.

Philip Because we have something he's never had.

There's a silence. Philip looks at her and nods, as if knowing he's right.

Nadia And?

Philip And what?

Nadia And even if that's true, why would I leave you?

Philip doesn't answer.

What possible reason would I have to leave you?

Philip is quiet, regretful.

Philip I had the idea we were perfectly aligned. When we met. We both have the same way of looking at the world. What you might call, a basically helpful attitude. We'd die rather than say so, but don't we both have this thing about trying to help?

Nadia So?

Philip It's odd. You've travelled more than I have. You've seen much more. But you still believe the world's all about argument and reason. You're power-blind. It's so obvious: he's trying to exert power over you. It's like there's a dimension missing from the way you look at people. You trust their good intentions.

Nadia Don't you?

Philip When I read what you write – someone does this, so someone else does that. You simply don't see it, do you? You're an innocent.

Nadia I'm not an innocent.

Suddenly Philip's anger begins to show through.

Philip I was born to an unhappy couple, remember?
I woke up every morning, my parents were tearing each
other apart. I keep the peace. That's what I'm good at.
The conciliator. I've done it all my life.

Nadia Well?

Philip Until yesterday evening. I warned you against him.
I said, be careful. I told you to be careful. You deliberately
ignored me.

Oliver returns with a tray.

Oliver It's a text message. We're losing her.

Nadia Who's that?

Oliver A patient. I'm losing a patient. It's been clear for
a while.

Philip is firm, a new resolution in his manner.

Philip I was just about to suggest to Nadia it might be
nice if we tried to get going.

Nadia What?

Philip I think we should get going. As we're all up. Why
not?

Oliver Philip . . .

Nadia Can we be practical? Where are you going?

Philip has turned to go out.

Philip I'm going to pack.

Nadia Pack?

Philip Yes. Pack. Pack now. I was thinking that way we'll
get to see something we wouldn't otherwise see. The road
to Harlech is spectacular at this time of day.

Philip has gone. Oliver is quietly clearing the table of last night's dishes onto the tray. Nadia looks across, hopeless.

Oliver I'm sorry. I'm not sure how, but I know this must be my fault.

Nadia It's so stupid. I can't take it seriously.

Oliver Nevertheless.

Oliver waits.

Nadia I should go to him.

Oliver Yes.

Nadia goes out. Nadia's voice is heard calling.

Nadia (*off*) Philip! Philip! Are you really packing? Philip! Do you have any idea of the time?

Oliver stands alone. Now dawn has broken, and the sun's rays are falling across the table. Oliver looks out for a few moments. Then he dials a number on his mobile phone.

Oliver Yes, it's Doctor Lucas. How's she doing? I see. It's all right. I'll be down soon. I know, but I'd like to.

Oliver listens for a moment.

Please don't concern yourself. It's my job.

Oliver clicks the little phone shut. Nadia returns, more amused than upset.

How is he?

Nadia Not good. He won't speak to me.

Oliver You're joking. Have another.

Nadia No thanks.

Oliver has nodded at the wine bottle.

He's packed. He's coming. I will have to leave.

Oliver I know.

Nadia It's better.

Oliver Yes. Undoubtedly.

Philip reappears.

Philip I'm ready.

Nadia Good. Let me go and get my things.

Nadia goes out. Philip is apprehensive.

Oliver Philip. What is this? Explain to me. You're angry with me. But why? It was chance. I just happened to be sitting on the lawn.

Philip In the middle of the night?

Oliver Yes. I was reading a book on linguistics.

There's a silence.

People are beginning to feel it may be the key to consciousness.

Philip And it's coincidence, is it?

Oliver What's coincidence?

Philip That she just happens to get up from my bed?

Oliver That. Yes. Coincidence.

Philip And you discussed me?

Oliver Briefly. But not exclusively. We discussed others as well.

Philip Why did you talk to her? Why did you have to talk to her, Dad?

Oliver looks at him.

Oliver Philip, I am not Lucifer. I don't wish you ill.

Philip I didn't say you were.

Oliver You can spend your whole life being angry with your father. It's a waste. Truly.

Philip is listening now.

Who do you want to be thinking about on your deathbed?

Philip I don't want to be on my deathbed.

Oliver No, well, nor do I. Nor does anyone.

Philip So?

Oliver In the normal sequence of things, it's a bad sign if you lie on your deathbed thinking about your father! That is not a sign of a life well lived. I would say if you're still thinking about your father, you've got real problems.

Philip I won't be.

Oliver Good.

Philip Don't flatter yourself. I won't!

There is a moment's silence. Oliver is quiet.

Oliver You ought to plan to be thinking of her.

Philip looks, only half daring to trust him.

I mean it. She's worth it.

Philip All right.

Oliver She's worth a whole lifetime.

Philip Really?

Oliver Yes. That's my opinion. It's my opinion. If it's of any value to you.

Philip looks at him.

Philip You mean it? You really mean it?

Oliver Come on, she's a great woman. She's extraordinary. However, you're going to find she has what Americans call issues. She has unresolved issues. And she has some incredibly stupid ideas. But there you are. You can't have everything.

Philip What sort of ideas?

Oliver She thinks she can set her private life away to one side. In an admirable determination to get on with things which she regards as far more important. I've tried it. It's not going to work.

Philip You said that to her?

Oliver Of course not.

Philip What did you talk about?

Oliver Oh . . .

Philip Tell me.

Oliver Nothing much.

Philip Tell me. Please. Dad.

Philip nods.

Oliver Your mother. Iraq. The woman I killed. Politics. Solitude. Love.

Nadia returns, calm, humorous, fully dressed.

Nadia All right. I agree. We drive towards nowhere.

Oliver Very well.

Nadia I'm happy. Let's do it. Let's spend the day kicking our heels and feeling remorse. Harlech.

Oliver Have some coffee first. Let me get the stuff.

Philip Dad . . .

Oliver Let me. I'd like to. At least have something before you set off.

He goes. Nadia and Philip are left alone.

Nadia I'm sorry.

Philip No. No, it's me who should be sorry. I don't know what happened. I thought he was trying to seduce you. I apologise. We can stay if you like.

Nadia says nothing.

I feel foolish.

Nadia Don't.

Nadia looks at him, then makes a decision.

I think you're right. We should go.

They move together, and kiss. They stand holding on to each other. They look into each other's eyes. Then they part. Neither knows what to do. It's resolved, but it's not. Some moments go by.

Philip, I didn't mean to hurt you.

Philip You didn't hurt me. Really.

Philip smiles.

Nadia I like your father.

Philip Good.

Philip waits for an answer but, before she can, Oliver returns with a tray of cups and a cafetière.

Oliver Here we are. Let's have the coffee. Then I have to go and watch someone die.

Philip Really? Do you have to? Why do you have to?

Oliver Because I said I would.

Nadia Seems like a good reason.

Oliver The best.

Oliver fusses over the cups and saucers. A few moments go by, everyone struck by the strangeness of the situation.

Anyone take sugar?

Nadia holds up her hand. Oliver spoons some into her cup.

Philip, you always took milk.

They smile at one another. He hands them both coffee.

Good. Excellent.

Oliver looks out at the hills.

What a splendid morning.

The three stand, nervously drinking their coffee.

Nadia We'll drive carefully.

Oliver Please do.

NINE

Oliver, alone.

Oliver I walked down the hill. I sat at my patient's bedside all day. She was tougher than I thought. My beeper was going. But years ago I learnt: deal with one thing at a time. My patient lost life some time early that evening. I'd told her the truth and I'd stayed with her to the end.

For some time, I heard nothing from Philip, nothing from Nadia. In fact, next time I read Nadia's name it was in another context entirely. When I saw what it was, forgive me, it made me smile.

TEN

Nadia's office. Nadia is once more casually dressed. Opposite her is Terri Scholes, an African-American, just twenty. She has not taken her jacket off. Nadia is holding an essay in her hand. She is passionate, disbelieving.

Nadia All right. I don't know. Really. I'm lost for a response. You're an intelligent student. You're much more than that. You're a highly intelligent person. What are you actually saying? Have you thought about it? Is this what you think? Not, 'I've got to do an essay, so I'd better write something.' But, 'I actually *believe* this. This – this is what I believe'?

Nadia holds the essay out, quoting.

'Why did Bush go to war? Because he could.' What kind of a statement is that? 'Because he knew he'd get away with it.' Do you call that a theory? 'For Bush and those like him, the exercise of power is enough in itself. Iraq was irrelevant to the war on terror. The point of the action was its very arbitrariness. To demonstrate to any possible enemy of the US that no one should ever consider themselves safe.'

Nadia smiles and holds the pages out to Terri.

Yeah, well, it's an interesting thesis, but, unburdened by evidence, maybe it doesn't quite have the impact you hope.

Nadia waits, but Terri is not responding.

I mean, Terri, this isn't a talk show. This isn't talk radio. It's not, 'Let's go into the studio and say stupid things.' This is an essay. In a serious discipline. The causes and origins of the war in Iraq.

Nadia shakes her head.

Jesus, I hear this stuff – as you do. I don't know what's happened. Suddenly everyone's a blowhard. Yale – the point of Yale University is – very simply – that it should be a blowhard-free zone.

Nadia quickly corrects herself.

By which – look, I'm not calling you a blowhard.

Terri Thanks.

Nadia I understand there's such a thing as disaffection. It's great. Why do students all have thick curtains? So they can sit in the dark and relish the gloom. In the nineteenth century there was a movement in Russia called nihilism. Have you heard of it?

Terri Sure.

Nadia I think you have.

Terri I've heard of it.

Nadia That's the irony. Of all my students, you're one of the few who would even know what it was. But truly, they should find you an application form. Do you remember what it was they believed in?

Terri Nothing.

Nadia They believed in nothing! Exactly!

Terri Random acts of violence.

Nadia Right. Do you?

Terri No, I don't. Not the violence.

Nadia OK. Good. So just the believing-in-nothing. Terri, there's a darkness in this essay. There's a scary kind of hopelessness. Are you going to tell me what's going on?

There's a moment's silence.

Terri All right. I'll tell you.

Nadia Thank you.

Terri For a couple of weeks now, I've been breaking up with my boyfriend.

Nadia Say what?

Terri My boyfriend's left me.

Nadia frowns.

Nadia Well, I'm sorry. I don't know what to say. I'm sorry.

Terri Not as sorry as me.

They both smile.

Nadia No.

Terri And losing him . . .

Nadia Yes?

Terri Losing him . . . it's made me think hard. It's made me realise a whole heap of things.

Nadia About American foreign policy?

Terri No. No, not about that. More about – more about, really, how I don't want to stay on at Yale.

Nadia Terri . . .

Terri I don't want to. Not without him.

Nadia looks in disbelief.

Nadia Oh come on . . .

Terri No, I'm serious.

Nadia I know you are. That's why I'm indignant.

Terri It's what I feel.

Nadia It may be what you feel.

Terri It is. It is what I feel.

Nadia I can't believe someone as gifted as you is seriously thinking of quitting solely because of some boy.

Terri He isn't 'some boy'.

Nadia No.

Terri He's not just 'some boy'.

Nadia I'm sorry.

Terri How would you like it if I talked about someone you knew and called him 'some boy'?

Nadia I shouldn't have said that. I apologise.

There's a silence.

Terri I met him more or less the first day I got here.

Nadia And?

Terri Just one example: every brick in this place reminds me of him.

Terri is a little teary, vulnerable.

OK, maybe it's part of the problem, I didn't bother to make other friends. I didn't need to. And some of the people I did meet didn't exactly make me want to meet any more.

Nadia No.

Terri And also – I don't want to walk out on campus and see him with somebody else. So, the point of all this: I put a lot of work in that essay. It's serious. It may be the last thing I write.

Nadia looks at her, thoughtful.

Nadia No, it's just . . . Look – I'm not your counsellor, I'm your teacher.

Terri It's fine. You can't hurt me. I've been hurt enough already.

Nadia takes another nervous, speculative look.

Nadia Just: I have some idea what you're going through.

Terri You do?

Nadia By an interesting coincidence, this summer I broke up with someone as well.

Terri Why?

Nadia Why? Well, we went on a ridiculous visit to Wales – or rather the bit beside Wales. He and I had been pretty close and yet for some reason, when I started talking with his father . . . I guess I began to see the son differently. Do you think that's unfair?

Terri Well, it is unfair, isn't it?

Nadia I don't think so.

Terri Was his father trying to break you up?

Nadia That's what my boyfriend believed.

Terri That's what I'd believe.

Nadia Yeah. But I didn't feel that. I really don't think he was. I was only there one night. We sat out on the lawn. It was like I'd been revealed to myself.

Terri And what was revealed?

Nadia I felt my own cowardice. He made me feel I'd been cowardly. In all sorts of ways. I'd made easy, cowardly choices. And also: I had this conviction – for as long as I stayed with Philip, I couldn't be true to myself.

Terri looks at her, unconvinced.

Terri Yeah, well, there's a difference, isn't there?

Nadia What difference?

Terri You were with the wrong man.

Nadia I don't know.

Terri And I was with the right one. It does make a difference.

Nadia Yes. Yes, it's just . . . Reading your essay, which perhaps I now begin to understand, I have this uneasy feeling that you may have been doing what psychologists call 'projecting' your unhappiness onto the subject in hand. We have to fight this, we have to make this not about ourselves, we have to fight our own feelings, we must try and be objective.

Terri I think I am. I'm not that stupid.

Nadia I've never said you were stupid.

Terri I know we're looking at two different things. First thing – my boyfriend has gone off with a girl who looks as if she eats shit with a dirty spoon, and also – second thing – I'm deeply despairing of the direction my government has recently been taking. I think I can hold both these things in my head at one time.

Nadia Yes, of course . . .

Terri Without confusing them!

Nadia I'm not saying you're confusing them. All I'm saying is – *look*!

Both of them have raised their voices.

I suppose I feel this so passionately – it's terribly important you don't simply give up.

Nadia picks the essay up again.

You say here, 'There is only one truth. The powerful exploit the powerless. Indiscriminately,' you say. 'And without any conscience. Rich countries are, by definition, massively self-interested and will never reach out to help anyone else. Whoever heard of a country,' you ask, 'which gave up power or wealth voluntarily? Nothing ever changes except by the use of force. Reason never prevails.'

Nadia throws it down.

I just ask: how can you write that?

Terri Because I've just lived through the last five years. I read the papers. I watch television. It's what I've seen for myself.

Nadia You're twenty, Terri. What are you suggesting? Everything's cynicism, is it – already?

Terri No. But why pretend? Why argue for things which aren't going to happen? Like the world getting any more sensible?

Nadia Because we have no other choice!

Nadia has yelled out in anger, way beyond the demands of the situation. Realising this, she moves across the room and speaks more quietly.

This is what gets to me. Despair's an affectation. That's what I think. It's self-indulgence.

Terri I don't think so. It's more like not fooling yourself.

Nadia looks at her, then goes and sits down at her desk.

Nadia I don't know. You must do what you think best. Please don't do it unthinkingly. All I'm saying is: just be careful. Delay any decision.

Terri Well, I will.

Nadia In either context. Your studies or your private life. After all, he may come back to you.

They both smile.

Terri Thank you. Is that the end of the class?

Nadia I guess it is.

Terri I'm going to give it twenty-four hours and then see how I feel.

Nadia Well, that's sensible. Good.

Nadia holds out the discarded essay.

Take this. I don't want it.

Terri takes it from her and heads for the door. Nadia clicks on her desk lamp to prepare to work. Then she looks up.

Oh, and by the way, I should tell you, if you do decide to see out your time here at Yale, I'm afraid I won't be here to see it through with you.

Terri Are you going to teach somewhere else?

Nadia Not exactly. No.

Terri waits.

Terri Are you going to tell me?

Nadia I don't mind telling you.

Nadia looks at her a moment.

I used to be a war correspondent. Recently I've noticed I miss it. I'm going back to Iraq.

End of Act Two.